DATE			

THE ENGLISH MORALITY AND RELATED DRAMA

A Bibliographical Survey

The English Morality and Related Drama
A BIBLIOGRAPHICAL SURVEY

Peter J. Houle

ARCHON BOOKS
1972

Library of Congress Cataloging in Publication Data

Houle, Peter J.
 The English morality and related drama.

 Bibliography: p.
 1. Moralities, English—History and criticism. I. Title.
PR643.M7H6 822'.051 70-38714
ISBN 0-208-01264-8

To Professor Charlotte Spivack

CONTENTS

PREFACE

The English Morality and Related Drama: A Bibliographical Survey is divided into three sections. The first section of the work gives individual treatment to each English morality. The plays are listed alphabetically. When possible, pertinent facts of original publication are given. These are followed by a listing of only the most available or the most important editions of the play in question. An asterisk is placed before the edition used in preparing the summary of the play. References to frequently cited collections of plays are abbreviated. The full citation of the collection can be found under the heading "Collections" immediately preceeding the first section. Full titles and dates are derived from Bernard Spivack's *Shakespeare and the Allegory of Evil,* pp. 483-493 and from Halliwell's *Dictionary of Old English Plays.* The dramatis personae of each play and any accompanying remarks that the title page may contain are given as they appear in the edition used, except that in many cases the spelling of the names of characters has been normalized to avoid confusion. For the most part the characters were listed on title pages in the order of their coming on stage, or, for some late plays, according to the scheme of doubling to be used in acting. The suggestions for doubling found on early title pages are often faulty. The student interested in doubling must refer to one of the modern treatments of this subject for accurate examinations of individual plays. The length of each play is given. Next follows a summary of the play. Summaries are seldom interesting to read and rarely interesting to write, especially when there are fifty-nine pieces to be summarized. It was not my intention to interpret any of these plays; consequently, my summaries at the risk of being colorless are purposly straight-forward and unembellished with editorial comment. In writing a few lines of comment on each play, I have limited myself nearly always to a statement of the main theme and the position of the play in the morality canon.

The following definitions may be helpful to a reader of my comments:

"full-scope" morality: a play presenting the history of typical man throughout his entire life on earth culminating in divine judgement. Such a play is structured after the medieval allegory of the Psychomachia, has for its dramatis personae personified abstractions or universalized types, and is primarily concerned with enacting in visible terms, and according to Christian doctrine, the moral progression of human life.

"estates" morality: a social play in which the different classes or professions in society are represented by characters to illustrate the health of the state or the relations of the classes among themselves.

"virtue" play: a play whose purpose is to inspire the audience to a particular virtue or set of virtues, such as Chastity or Patience. The positive example in all the English "virtue" plays is invested in a feminine role.

"hybrid" play: a play based on persons from history, the Bible, or legend but containing as well personified abstractions borrowed from the morality drama.

"youth" play: a play concerned with the proper rearing of children and with those faults to which children and young adults are especially prone. These plays were often written expressly to be acted by students themselves.

"Mankind" figure: the character representing all humanity, whose confrontation with vice and virtue constitutes the principal action of the morality. The Mankind figure may be "split" or "bifurcated", that is, divided into two figures, one who follows the path of virtue and the other who follows that of vice.

"the Vice": the leader of the forces of evil, always an able and constant intriguer, and a humorist boastful of his skill and duplicity.

Finally, in Section I a bibliography of criticism on each play is given under the heading "Critical Studies." There are some plays with no such heading. This means that to my knowledge there has been no article or book solely devoted to that play. In this case, it is most probable that the reader will find additional information on the play in question by checking in the leading full length studies of the morality and Tudor drama listed toward the end of this introduction. Also, the editions of many plays often provide in their introductions useful critical material.

Section II of this bibliographical survey consists of six appendices dealing with topics related to the morality drama.

Section III of the survey is a listing of critical material on the morality drama. Only works dealing with the moralities in general are here included; articles on an individual play will be found under the entry for that play in Section I. It must be stressed that both the general and individual bibliographies are not intended to be exhaustive listings of everything ever written about the moralities. My intention was simply to list for the beginning researcher of the morality drama as many useful articles and books as possible.

Some bibliographical entries are included in all three sections. For example, Southern's *Medieval Theatre in the Round* will be found first under the entry for *The Castle of Perseverance* (No. V) with which it deals in detail, second, under Appendix VI, the Staging of Morality Plays, and third, in the general bibliography. Although some repetition of entries results, this method of listing minimizes tedious cross-references.

The student beginning a study of the morality drama or that of the Sixteenth Century should be directed to several major works whose aid cannot help being considerable to anyone. One of the first and still best treatments of the morality drama is the hundred-page essay by E. N. S. Thompson, *The English Moral Play.* The staging of moralities is treated in David Bevington's *From Mankind to Marlowe,* in Southern's *Medieval Theatre in the Round,* and Wickham's *Early English Stages 1300-1660.* A second study by Bevington entitled *Tudor Drama and Politics* deals effectively with the role of the theater in the complex political and religious arena of the Sixteenth Century. Valuable also is *The Tudor Interlude* by T. W. Craik, and, of course, Chambers' *The Medieval Stage and The Elizabethan Stage*. The finest contemporary consideration of the morality drama and its relation to the later Elizabethan drama is Bernard Spivack's *Shakespeare and the Allegory of Evil*.

I wish to gratefully acknowledge the English Department at the University of Massachusetts for a fellowship for independent study which enabled me to write this Survey. Thanks are given in particular to several of the English faculty. Professor Vernon Helming patiently read the first draft of this survey and saved it from many inaccuracies. Professor Arthur Kinney has given valuable bibliographical advice. Professor Bernard Spivack has offered continual encouragement and expert instruction. I wish to especially acknowledge Professor Charlotte Spivack with whom I have had the privilege of studying the Tudor and Elizabethan drama. Professor Spivack first suggested my writing a survey of the morality drama and has helped in every stage of its preparation.

P. J. H.

Amherst, Massachusetts

ABBREVIATIONS

AN&Q	*American Notes and Queries*
AngBbl	*Anglia Beiblatt*
AnM	*Annuale Medievale*
Archiv	*Archiv für das Studium der neueren Sprachen und Literaturen*
BB	*Bulletin of Bibliography*
BSUF	*Ball State University Forum*
CD	*Comparative Drama*
CE	*College English*
CentR	*Centennial Review*
CL	*Comparative Literature*
CP	*Classical Philology*
CR	*Classical Review*
DA	*Dissertation Abstracts*
EA	*Etudes Anglaises*
ELN	*English Language Notes*
EngSt	*Englische Studien*
ES	*English Studies*
HLQ	*Huntington Library Quarterly*
ILN	*Illustrated London News*
JEGP	*Journal of English and Germanic Philology*
JGE	*Journal of General Education*
Mag	*Magnificat*
MLN	*Modern Language Notes*
MLQ	*Modern Language Quarterly*
MLR	*Modern Language Review*
MP	*Modern Philology*
MQ	*Mississippi Quarterly*
MS	*Medieval Studies* (Toronto)
N&Q	*Notes and Queries*
NR	*New Republic*
PBSA	*Papers of the Bibliographical Society of America*
PMLA	*Publications of the Modern Language Association*
PQ	*Philological Quarterly*

QQ	*Queen's Quarterly*
RenD	*Reniassance Drama*
RES	*Review of English Studies*
RN	*Renaissance News*
RORD	*Research Opportunities in Renaissance Drama*
SAB	*Shakespeare Association Bulletin*
SEL	*Studies in English Literature, 1500-1900*
SELit	*Studies in English Literature* (University of Tokyo)
SP	*Studies in Philology*
SQ	*Shakespeare Quarterly*
SSL	*Studies in Scottish Literature* (University of South Carolina)
TA	*Theatre Annual*
ThS	*Theater Survey*
TLS	*Times Literary Supplement*
TN	*Theatre Notebook*
TNTL	*Tijdschrift voor Nederlandse Taal-en Letterkunde*
TSE	*Tulane Studies in English*
UTSE	*University of Texas Studies in English*
UVS	*University of Virginia Studies*
ZDP	*Zeitschrift für deutche Philologie*

COLLECTIONS

Adams	Joseph Quincy Adams. *Chief Pre-Shakes-pearean Dramas.* Boston: Houghton and Mifflin, 1924.
Brandl	Alois Brandl. *Quellen des weltlichen Dramas in England vor Shakespeare.* In Quellen und Forschungen zur Sprach und Culturge-schichte des germanischen Volker, LXXX. Strassburg, 1898.
Dodsley	Robert Dodsley. *A Select Collection of Old English Plays.* 15 vols. 4th ed. rev. W. C. Hazlett. London, 1874-76. (Re-printed, New York: B. Blom, 1964).
EETS	Publications of the *Early English Text Society.* London, 1864 to date.
Farmer	John S. Farmer. *Six Anonymous Plays.* London, 1905. (Reprinted, New York: Barnes and Noble, 1966).
	_____. *Six Anonymous Plays.* London, 1906. (Reprinted, New York: Barnes and Noble, 1966).
	_____. *Recently Recovered "Lost" Tudor Plays.* London, 1907. (Reprinted, New York: Barnes and Noble, 1966).
	_____. *Five Anonymous Plays.* London, 1908. (Reprinted, New York: Barnes and Noble, 1966).
	Plays from the Farmer series will be listed under "Editions" under the year of first publication. For example, Farmer, 1908 refers to *Five Anonymous Plays.*
Jahrbuch	*Jahrbuch der deutschen Shakespeare-Gesellschaft.* Berlin, 1864 to date.
MSR	*Malone Society Reprints.* London: Publica-tions of the Malone Society, 1907 to date.

Manly   John M. Manly. *Specimens of the Pre-*
             Shakespearean Drama. 2 vols. Boston:
             Ginn and Co., 1897. (Reprinted, New
             York: Dover Publications, 1967).
Materialien   *Materialien zur Kunde des alteren englischen*
             Dramas. Louvain, 1902-14. Continued as
             Materials for the Study of the Old English
             Drama. 1927-58.

THE ENGLISH MORALITY AND RELATED DRAMA

A Bibliographical Survey

I. ALBION KNIGHT, 1537-65
(Anonymous)

The title page, date, and name of printer are missing. The play was entered in the books of the Stationers' Company for 1565-66 under the title *a merye playe bothe pythy and pleasant of albyon knyghte.*

Editions
J. P. Collier. *Shakespeare Society Papers,* I, 1844.
*Farmer, 1906.
W. W. Greg. *Malone Society Collections,* I, 3. 1909.

Dramatis Personae

Albion Knight	
Injury	These appear in the
Justice	fragment.
Division	
Principality	
Peace	
Maintenance	These are mentioned but do
Rest	not appear.
Old Debate	
Double-Device	
Dame Plenty	

Length of the fragment: 408 lines.

Plot Summary
The fragment of *Albion Knight* begins in medias res. In an argument concerning the judgment of a man by his looks, Justice criticizes the Vice Injury's "light apparel." When Injury (alias Manhood) retorts with the familiar quotation "Nolite judicare secundum faciem," Justice still maintains that apparel may indicate frailness, pride, or instability. At the intervention of Albion Knight (England) the two

3

discontinue their quarrel and are made to swear a pact of friendship with Albion. Injury convinces Albion of the sorry state of a realm where the law favors the Principality (monarchy). Justice suggests that he and Injury work for a correction of current evils, and Albion heartily seconds the project.

Alone on the stage, Injury, in lines typical of the Vice, proudly reveals to the audience that he is not Manhood at all, but Injury. He boasts of the trouble he will cause — the destruction of Justice and the exile of Peace from Albion Knight. He elicits the help of Division, who, armed with sword, dagger, bill, and buckler indicative of his disruptive role, speaks several frenzied lines much like an incantation. Injury explains that Albion has sent Justice to influence the Principality and himself on a similar mission to the Lords Temporal, and that he has stalled on his errand to ask advice of Division. Division promptly declares that the efforts of Peace between the Commons and Principality will come to nought because Double-Device will cause the King (Principality) to think that the Commons spitefully refuse to give him money in time of need. On the other hand, Double-Device will allow the Commons to believe that the King acts only to enrich himself. Also, a second evil agent, Old-Debate, will see that the Lords Spiritual wrangle with the Lords Temporal concerning who should wield power. The nobles will accuse the clergy men of being lowborn and newcomers, and the prelates will derive from their learning and sanctity a just cause why they should rule.

A third plot is hatched to effect a permanent separation of Albion Knight from Dame Plenty (his intended wife) and from Rest and Peace. Division, posing as Policy, will go to Albion with the message that Injury has failed in his mission among the Lords Temporal. Division will then advise the confused Albion to begin a life of mirth and prodigality. The fragment breaks off here.

Comments

Albion Knight is a social morality concerning the impasse which existed about 1537 between King Henry VIII and his lowborn advisers on one side and the nobility and commons on the other.

Other "social" plays:

> *All for Money* (No. II).
> *Impatient Poverty* (No. XVIII).
> *Liberality and Prodigality* (No. XXIII).
> *Like Will to Like* (No. XXV).
> *Wealth and Health* (No. LV).

See *Cobbler's Prophesy* (No. VII) for a list of the "estates" plays, all of which are social pieces.

Critical Studies

Dodds, Madeline. "The Date of *Albion Knight.*" The Library, 3rd ser. 4:157-170 (1913).

Jones, Gwen Ann. "The Political Significance of the Play of *Albion Knight.*" *JEGP*, 17:267-280 (1918).

II. ALL FOR MONEY, 1559-77
(Thomas Lupton)

A moral and Pitieful Comedie, Intituled, All for Money. Plainly representing the maners of men, and fashion of the world noweadays. Compiled by T. Lupton. Roger Warde and Richard Mundee, 1578.

Editions

J. O. Halliwell. *Literature of the Sixteenth and Seventeenth Centuries Illustrated.* London, 1851.

*E. Vogel. *Jahrbuch,* XL. 1904.

II

Dramatis Personae
 Theology
 Science
 Art
 Money
 Adulation
 Mischievous Help
 Pleasure
 Pressed for Pleasure
 Sin
 Swift to Sin
 Damnation
 Satan
 Pride
 Gluttony
 Learning with Money

Learning without Money
Money without Learning
All for Money
Neither Money nor Learning
Moneyless and Fiendless
Gregory Graceless
William-with-the-Two-Wives
Nichol [Never-out-of-Law]
Sir Laurence [Livingless]
Mother Croote
Judas
Dives
Godly Admonition
Virtue
Humility
Charity

Length of the play: 1,572 lines.

Plot Summary

Theology, Science, and Art testify that men study them only to gain money and not for knowledge of God or for utility to man. At the entrance of Money a genealogy of evil unfolds involving not a little stage ingenuity. Aided by Mischievous Help and Adulation, Money vomits forth Pleasure by means of "some fine conveyance . . . from beneath." Pleasure in his turn feels sick and with the help of Pressed for Pleasure spews forth Sin, the Vice. Swift to Sin and Pressed for Pleasure next deliver Sin of Damnation "who shall have a terrible vysard on his face and his garment shalbe painted with flames of fire." All leave but Sin, who then meets and argues with Satan. Pride and Gluttony persuade Sin not to forsake Satan, who has apparently mistreated him in the past. After the Devils depart, Sin leaves to seek out his grandfather Money. A debate in the Heywood fashion follows between Learning with Money, Learning without Money, Money without Learning, and Neither Money nor Learning. Although this scene has no connection with the dramatic action of the play, it does make a positive statement about money and provides a follow-up of ideas hinted at in the Prologue — that money may be used for good, that it must be subject to reason and learning, and that it is certainly not necessary for happiness.

Money and Sin set up in business their most avid human disciple, All for Money, who, dressed as a magistrate, is much disposed to rule favorably on any suit accompanied by a generous donation. With Sin as usher he first awards freedom to Gregory Graceless in payment of £100, one-half the amount taken in a theft and subsequent murder for which Gregory is about to be hanged. Next, for more than £100 All for Money promises a jury decision of not-guilty for a young girl accused of murdering her bastard child. Moneyless and Friendless, who has been victimized by a rich man, is sent away guilty for reasons implicit in his name. Another suitor, William-with-the-Two-Wives, is granted freedom from the shrewish first wife to marry the more desirable second. William must pay forty old angels and a yearly capon at Christmas to the accommodating judge. Nichol-Never-out-of-Law is granted a piece of land belonging to a neighbor, and a sixth suitor, the old and very ignorant Popish priest Sir Laurence Livingless, becomes chaplain to All for Money. The last suitor, Mother Croote, "an hundredth yeres olde," blind but still lusty, is permitted to buy two false witnesses to testify to her betrothal to a handsome young man. When All for Money leaves for the day, Sin points him out as an example of one quickly falling into the clutches of Damnation. Two damned souls from the past, Judas and Dives, offer still another case history of the fruits of avarice. They lament their greed and are driven to hell by Damnation. Virtue, Humility, Charity, and Godly Admonition end the play with a final statement of its message and a prayer for Elizabeth, her Counsel, the Lords and Commons.

Comments

All for Money, a social morality, has little dramatic unity; except for the Vice Sin, his grandfather Money, and Damnation, the thirty-one characters appear only once each. Sin's role as usher to All for Money is similar to that of Merry Report in Heywood's *Weather* (No. LVI).

Other "social" plays:
> *Albion Knight* (No. I).
> *Impatient Poverty* (No. XVIII).
> *Liberality and Prodigality* (No. XXIII).
> *Like Will to Like* (No. XXV).
> *Wealth and Health* (No. LV).

See *Cobbler's Prophesy* (No. VII) for a list of the "estates" plays, all of which are social pieces.

See Heywood's *Play of the Weather* (No. LVI) and *Play of Love* (No. XXVIII) for two earlier examples of the "debate" on the stage.

Critical Studies

Craik, T. W. "Some notes on Thomas Lupton's *All for Money." N&Q,* 199:233-235 (1954).

III. APPIUS AND VIRGINIA, 1559-68
(R. B.)

A new Tragicall Comedie of Apius and Virginia, Wherein is liuely expressed a rare example of the vertue of Chastitie, by Virginias constancy, in wishing to be slaine at her owne Fathers handes, than to be deflowred of the wicked Iudge Apius. By R. B. William How for Richard Jones, 1575.

Editions
Dodsley, IV.
*Farmer, 1908.
R. B. McKerrow. *MSR*, 1911.

Dramatis Personae

Virginius	Conscience	[Fame]
Mater	Justice	
Virginia	Claudius	
Haphazard	Rumour	
Mansipulus	Comfort	
Mansipula	Reward	
Subservus	Doctrina	
Appius	Memory	

Length of the play: 1,216 lines.

Plot Summary

The Prologue announces that the play to follow will be an example not only for maidens but also for married women as well. The first scene depicts a model family — the virtuous father Virginius, his wife, and their dutiful and chaste daughter Virginia. Under the instigation of the Vice, Haphazard, the wicked Judge Appius plots how he may enjoy Virginia. Unmoved by the pleas of Justice and Conscience, Appius sends the corrupt courtier Claudius to summon Virginius as a first step to Virginia. A false trial ensues in which Claudius testifies that sixteen years earlier Virginius had stolen a thrall from him and brought her up as his own daughter. Appius rules that Virginia be brought immediately into his custody. Rumour calls for the destruction of both Claudius and Appius. Rather than submit to Appius, Virginia seeks remedy in death by decapitation at the hands of her father. Prompted by Comfort, Virginius offers to Appius the head of his daughter. Justice and Reward condemn Appius to prison, where he commits suicide. Claudius is granted mercy at the demand of

Virginius, and Haphazard is led off to be hanged. Fame, Doctrina, and Memory attend to the funeral rites of Virginia. The Epilogue emphasizes the example of Virginia's chastity.

Comments

Appius and Virginia is a "virtue" play of the hybrid group. The only allegorical figure of importance is the Vice, Haphazard. He not only victimizes Appius and the servants, but offers some of the best documentation of the Vice's role as deceiver of all classes.

Other "virtue" plays:

>*Godly Queen Hester* (No. XIV).
>*Life and Repentance of Mary Magdalene* (No. XXIV).
>*Patient and Meek Grissell* (No. XLII).
>*Virtuous and Godly Susanna* (No. LIV).

See Coming of Death (Appendix I).

Critical Studies

Ekiblad, Inga-Stina. "Storm Imagery in *Appius and Virginia.*" *N&Q,* 3:5-7 (1956).

Happé, P. "Tragic Themes in Three Tudor Moralities." *SEL,* 5:207-227 (1965). [Discussion of *Cambises* (No. IV), *Horestes* (No. XVII), and *Appius and Virginia.*]

Rumbour, Otto. *Die Geschichte von Appius und Virginia in der englischen Litteratur.* Breslau, 1890.

IV. CAMBISES, 1558-69
(Thomas Preston)

A lamentable tragedy mixed ful of pleasant mirth, conteyning the life of Cambises king of Percia, from the beginning of his kingdome vnto his death, his one good deed of execution, after that many wicked deeds and tirannous murders, committed by and through him, and last of all, his odious death by Gods Iustice appointed. By Thomas Preston. John Allde, n.d.

Editions
T. Hawkins. *Origin of the English Drama,* I. London, 1773.
Dodsley, IV.
*Manly, II.
Adams.
Baskervill, Heltzel, and Nethercot. *Elizabethan and Stuart Plays.* New York, 1934.

Dramatis Personae

Counsel		Cambises	For one
Huf		Epilogue	Man.
Praxaspes	For one	Prologue	
Murder	Man.	Sisamnes	
Lob		Diligence	
Third Lord		Cruelty	For one
[Fourth] Lord		Hob	Man.
Ruf		Preparation	
Commons Cry	For one	First Lord	
Commons Complaint	Man.	Ambidexter	For one
Lord Smirdis		Trial	Man.
Venus		Meretrix	
Knight		Shame	
Snuf		Otian	For one
Small Hability		Mother	Man.
Proof	For one	Lady	
Execution	Man.	Queen	
Attendance		Young Child	For one
Second Lord		Cupid	Man.

11

Length of the play: 1,255 lines.

Plot Summary

Once the Prologue has affirmed that God does not allow a tyrant to rule for long, the newly enthroned Cambises of Persia, with the aid of his counsellors, delegates his authority to the judge Sisamnes while the King campaigns in Egypt. The action then turns to Ambidexter, the Vice, who effectively demonstrates the double-dealing implicit in his name, when, posing as a miles gloriosus, he outwits the three ruffians Huf, Ruf, and Snuf. Ambidexter next convinces Sisamnes that by bribes he may assure that the King will not be informed of his administrative injustices. Thus, Sisamnes follows a policy of tyrannical rule which prefigures the later actions of his royal master. Commons Cry, along with Commons Complaint, Proof, and Trial convice the King of Sisamnes' guilt. Immediately invoking the death penalty in his one and only act of justice, Cambises commands that the guilty judge be executed and flayed before his son Otian, who will succeed his father as judge.

Commending the King for his speedy justice in avenging the Commons against Sisamnes, Praxaspes, a loyal councilor, suggests to Cambises that his rule would be more effective if he would curb his drinking. To show that he can act and think straight while under the influence of wine, Cambises orders Praxaspes' young son to be brought in and set up as a target. He promptly shoots the child through the heart as a proof that liquor has not benumbled his senses. In a choral commentary Ambidexter condemns the murder and predicts even more infamy to come.

Ambidexter's double-dealing takes the form of counsel to Smirdis, the King's brother and heir, to wait patiently for the day when as King he may rule wisely. In an able demonstration of his ability to "play with both hands," Ambidexter then warns Cambises that Smirdis seeks the throne and his death. Faithful to his characteristic decisiveness, Cambises

sends the two murderers Cruelty and Murder to stab innocent
Smirdis to death. Ambidexter continues his knavery in
comic relief as he frightens two neighbors, Lob and Hob, and
then sets them to fighting. Marian-may-be-Good, Hob's wife,
succeeds in chasing the Vice off.

The action returns to Cambises in a last example of un-
reasoned use of power. Venus commands Cupid to wound the
heart of Cambises to love his lady-cousin. Although a marriage between cousins is forbidden, Cambises insists on the
wedding. When his new wife sees parallels in the fighting of
two young lions and the jealousy of Cambises for Smirdis,
she enrages the King so that he orders her death also.

Cambises downfall is soon to follow. Severely wounded in
a fall from his horse, he can find no one to help him, and he
also dies. Three Lords affirm that the King has received just
payment for his wickedness. The Epilogue prays that Queen
Elizabeth and her council may practice justice and truth.

Comments

Cambises is a hybrid play containing much of the spectacu-
lar that was to become so popular in Elizabethan drama. Although some of the minor characters appear in the Dramatis
Personae as abstractions, they are actually more realistic
figures than their names suggest.

Critical Studies

Allen, Don Cameron. "A Source for *Cambises.*" *MLN,*
49:384-387 (1934).
Armstrong, W. A. "The Authorship and Political Meaning of
Cambises." *ES,* 36:289-299 (1955).
——————"The Background and Sources of Preston's
Cambises." *ES,* 31:129-135 (1950).
Feldman, Abraham. "King Cambises' Vein." *N&Q,* 196-98-
100 (1951).
Happé, P. "Tragic Themes in Three Tudor Moralities." *SEL,*
5:207-227 (1965). [Discussion of *Cambises, Horestes*
(No. XVII), and *Appius and Virginia* (No. III).]

Johnson, Robert Carl. "Antedatings from *Cambises." N&Q,* 15:246 (1968).

_____ "Press Variants in *Cambises." N&Q,* 15:246-247 (1968).

_____ "The Third Quarto of *Cambises." N&Q,* 15:247 (1968).

_____ "Thomas Preston's *Cambises:* A Critical Edition." *DA,* 25:4688 (1965).

Linthicum, M. C. "The Date of *Cambyses." PMLA,* 49:959-961 (1934).

Starnes, D. T. "Richard Taverner's *The Garden of Wisdom,* Carion's *Chronicles,* and the Cambyses Legend." *UTSE,* 35:22-31 (1956).

V. THE CASTLE OF PERSEVERANCE, 1400-1425
(Anonymous)

Macro MS, now Folger MS.V. a. 354. First published by the EETS, 1904.

Editions
*F. J. Furnivall and A. W. Pollard. *EETS,* Extra Series, xci, London, 1904 (Reprinted, 1924).

J. S. Farmer. *The Turdor Facsimile Texts.* London and Edinburgh, 1908.

Adams (Abbreviated text).

Mark Eccles. *EETS,* No. 262, 1969.

Dramatis Personae
[See the Introduction to the Ramsay edition of Skelton's *Magnyfycence (EETS,* E. S., xcviii, p. clxxvii) for a grouping of the characters into Neutral, Good, and Evil. The following list gives the characters as they are grouped in the MS.]

14

Two Vexillatores (Flag-bearers).

Mundus (World) and with him Voluptas (Pleasure),
 Stulticia (Folly), Garcio (Boy Servant to World).

Belial (Devil) and with him Superbia (Pride), Ira (Wrath),
 Invidia (Envy).

Caro (Flesh) and with him Gula (Gluttony), Luxuria
 (Lechery), Accidia (Sloth).

Humanum Genus (Mankind) and with him Bonus Angelus
 (Good Angel), and Malus Angelus (Bad Angel).

Avaricia (Avarice or Covetise), Detraccio (Detraction or
 Backbiting), Confessio (Confession or Schrift),
 Penitencia (Penance).

Humilitas (Humility), Paciencia (Patience), Caritas (Love),
 Abstinencia (Abstinence), Castitas (Chastity), Solicitudo
 (Industry), Largitas (Generosity).

Mors (Death), Anima (Soul), Misericordia (Mercy), Veritas
 (Truth), Justicia (Justice), Pax (Peace).

Pater sedens in trono (God the Father on his throne).

(Stage directions call for the "iiij dowteris," the Four
 Daughters — Mercy, Truth, Justice, and Peace, to be
 dressed as follows: Mercy in white, Justice or Righteous-
 ness in red, Truth in green, and Peace in black. The MS
 gives the number of roles to be thirty-six, but the list
 names only thirty-five. Furnivall suggests that Veynglory,
 although he has no speaking role, was the thirty-sixth
 player.)

Length of the play: 3,650 lines.

Plot Summary

Spoken by two Vexillatores, the Introduction to the play
gives proper salutation to the audience, names the Vices and
Virtues operative in man's terrestrial existence, and gives a
brief resume of the play to come. The three Evil Powers
(Mundus, Caro, and Belial), Deus Pater, and Covetise are
placed each on a throne or scaffold around the playing area.

The audience first listens to the mighty potentate Mundus describe the extent of his domain and his indebtedness to his minion Avaricia. Self-descriptions are next spoken in turn by Belial and Caro, each on his own scaffold. Belial names Superbia, Ira, and Invidia as his companions; and Caro delights in Gula, Luxuria, and Accidia.

Flanked by Bonus Angelus and Malus Angelus, young Humanum Genus speaks of the helpless condition into which he was born and then faces the first major decision of his life — whether to follow the sensible but unattractive promptings of Bonus Angelus to a life of virtue, or to yield to the persuasive encouragements of Malus Angelus to a life of sin. Having decided on the sinful life, Humanum Genus is conducted to all three scaffolds, where he meets their vicious occupants. Before long, Humanum Genus has met and sworn allegiance to all three of the Evil Powers and has heard each of the Seven Deadly Sins give a suitable recitation of her evil doings in the world. With the help of Confessio and Penitencia, Bonus Angelus works the conversion of Humanum Genus, persuades him to repent of his ways, and prompts him to reconcile himself with God by the sacrament of Confession. Better to insure the continued fidelity of Humanum Genus, the virtues lodge him in the Castle of Perseverance.

The next scenes in the play derive from the *Psychomachia* of Prudentius. As soon as word is brought to the Evil Powers that Humanum Genus resides in the Castle of Perseverance, their army is mustered for an attack on the soul of their human victim. In the meantime, the forces of good, Caritas, Abstinencia, Castitas, Solicitudo, Largitas, and Humilitas assemble in preparation for the conflict. Led by Belial, the attack upon the Castle mounts two major offensives. At each assault the Vices are repulsed by means of roses — the emblems of the Passion of Christ. Realizing that an open attack is to no avail, Mundus summons Avaricia, who tricks Humanum Genus into covetousness, the sin of old age. Before Humanum Genus has time to enjoy the thousand marks given him by Avaricia, Mors comes to summon him before God. Garcio, the servant of Mundus, claims the thousand marks for his master; Humanum Genus is left with nothing but his sins. While Malus Angelus tries through mockery to distract his human victim, Humanum Genus dies praying to Misericordia.

The play ends with the debate of the Four Daughters (Mercy, Truth, Justice, and Peace) before the throne of God the Father. Justicia and Veritas argue for the letter of the law and the damnation of Humanum Genus; but Misericordia and Pax plead for his forgiveness. The decision of God the Father is merciful, and he is saved. The spectators are reminded to think on death and the Te Deum is sung.

Comments

The Castle of Perseverance is the finest example in England of the "full-scope" morality. Avaricia (Covetise) is the chief Vice. He has a scaffold with Belial, Caro, and Mundus. Largitas admits him to be the leader of the Seven Deadly Sins (11. 2454-66). Avaricia finally succeeds in seducing Humanum Genus after the others have failed.

See Coming of Death (Appendix I).
      Debate of the Body and Soul (Appendix II).
      Debate of the Heavenly Graces (Appendix III).
      The Devil in the Moralities (Appendix IV).
      Psychomachia (Appendix V).

Critical Studies

Allison, T. E. "On the Body and Soul Legend." *MLN*, 42:102-106 (1927).

Arnott, P. D. "The Origins of Medieval Theatre in the Round." *TN*, 15:84-87 (1961).

Bennett, Jacob. *"The Castle of Perseverance:* Redactions, Place, and Date." *MS*, 24:141-152 (1962).

———— "A Linguistic Study of *The Castle of Perseverance."* *DA*, 21:872 (1960).

Cornelius, Roberta D. *The Figurative Castle.* Bryn Mawr: Bryn Mawr Press, 1930.

Hammerle, K. *"The Castle of Perseverance and Pearl." Anglia,* 60; Neue Folge, 48:401-402 (1936).

Henry, Avril K. *"The Castle of Perseverance:* The Stage Direction at Line 1767." *N&Q,* 12:448 (1965).

Loomis, Roger Sherman. "Lincoln as a Dramatic Centre," in *Mélanges d'Histoire de Théâtre offerts à Gustave Cohen.* Paris: Librairie Nizet, 1950.

McCutchan, J. Wilson. "Covetousness in *The Castle of Perseverance." UVS,* 4:175-191 (1951).

_____ "Justice and Equity in the English Morality Play." *JHI,* 19:405-410 (1958).

Robinson, J. W. "Three Notes on Medieval Theatre." *TN,* 16:60-62 (1962).

Schell, Edgar T. "On the Imitation of Life's Pilgrimage in *The Castle of Perseverance." JEGP,* 67:235-248 (1968).

Schmitt, Natalie C. "Was there a Medieval Theatre in The Round? A Re-evaluation of the Evidence (Part I)." *TN,* 23:130-142 (1969). Part II, *TN,* 24:18-25 (1970).

Smart, Walter K. *"The Castle of Perseverance:* Place, Date, and a Source." In *The Manly Anniversary Studies in Language and Literature.* Chicago: University of Chicago Press (1923), pp. 42-53.

Southern, Richard. *The Medieval Theatre in the Round: A Study of the Staging of The Castle of Perseverance.* London: Faber and Faber, 1957.

Willis, James. "Stage Directions in *The Castle of Perseverance." MLR,* 51:404-405 (1956).

Withington, Robert. *"The Castle of Perseverance,* Line 695." *PQ,* 14:270 (1935).

VI. CLYOMON AND CLAMYDES, 1570-83
(Anonymous)

The Historie of the two valiant Knights, Syr Clyomon Knight of the Golden Sheeld, sonne to the King of Denmarke: And Clamydes the white Knight, sonne to the King of Suauia. As it hath been sundry times Acted by her Maiesties Players. Thomas Creede, 1599.

Editions
Alexander Dyce. *Works of George Peele,* III. London, 1828-39.
A. H. Bullen. *Works of George Peele,* II. London, 1888.
*W. W. Greg. *MSR,* 1913.
Littleton, Betty J. *Clyomon and Clamydes: A Critical Edition.* The Hague and Paris: Mouton, 1968.

Dramatis Personae
Clamydes, son to the King of Suavia
Juliana, daughter to the King of Denmark
Clyomon, son to the King of Denmark
Subtle Shift, the Vice
Two Lords attendant
Alexander the Great
A Lord Attendant
Brian Sans Foy
A Boatswain
Neronis, daughter to the King of the Strange Marshes
Two Lords Attendant
A Knight, released by Clamydes
Thrasellus, King of Norway
Two Lords Attendant
Rumor
Corin, a Shepherd
Providence
The Widow of the King of the Strange Marshes

19

A Page
The King of Denmark
The Queen of Denmark
A Lord Attendant
Knowledge
(Supernumeraries) A herald and a third Lord attendant on
the King of Suavia, soldiers of Alexander, two servants of
Brian Sans Foy, two Ladies attendant on Neronis, two
more knights released by Clamydes, a second Lord atten-
dant on the King of Denmark, Corin's dog.

Length of the play: 2,238 lines.

Plot Summary

To win the hand of Juliana, Clamydes vows to slay the
maiden-stealing flying serpent dwelling in the Forest of
Marvels. Because every man who would slay this serpent must
be a knight, Clamydes returns home to be dubbed. Clyomon,
Knight of the Golden Shield and Juliana's wandering brother,
hires Subtle Shift, the Vice (alias Knowledge), as a servant.
When they come by accident to the dubbing of Clamydes,
Clyomon cleverly maneuvers his own dubbing in Clamydes'
place and escapes. Subtle Shift is apprehended in flight and
readily offers his allegiance to the wronged Clamydes, who
must now revenge himself on Clyomon. They meet and
promise to return in fifteen days to fight before King Alexander of Macedonia. Although warned by Subtle Shift of the
Enchanter Brian Sans Foy who lives in the Forest of Marvels,
Clamydes resolves to slay the serpent in the fifteen days
intervening before the fight with Clyomon. Within five days
Clamydes has slain the serpent. But he has also become the
victim of Brian's spell, and is carried off to prison with the
other captured would-be husbands of Juliana.

Blown into a strange land by adverse weather, Clyomon,
now unable to keep his rendez-vous with Clamydes, takes
refuge with Neronis, daughter of King Petranius of the

Strange Marshes. Clamydes wakes on the fifteenth day, frees
three knights held by Brian, and hastens to Alexander's court.
Brian retains possession, however, of the silver shield which
was a gift from Juliana to Clamydes and also the serpent's
head which he was to use to win Juliana. Neronis has fallen in
love with Clyomon, but he must leave her to return to Alexander's court to meet Clamydes. When Clyomon learns that
Clamydes has also failed to appear on the fifteenth day, he
resolves to return to Neronis. Rumor informs him that King
Thrasellus of Norway has abducted Neronis. She, however,
has escaped the tyrant, and, posing as a servant, gains employment with the shepherd Corin. Clyomon confronts and slays
Thrasellus, buries him, and leaves his own golden shield as a
gravestone. Neronis almost commits suicide when she sees the
golden shield on the grave, but Providence points out to her
that it is, in fact, the wicked King who lies buried there and
not Clyomon.

In the meantime, Neronis' father has died of grief, and his
kingdom is now divided into two factions — that of his preg-
nant wife and that of his brother Mustantius. When a trial by
combat is agreed upon to decide which faction shall rule the
Strange Marshes, Clyomon and Clamydes offer themselves as
champions on opposing sides. Before the fight can take place,
a settlement is made, and, what is more, Clyomon reveals his
true identity as Juliana's brother and heir to the Danish
throne. Refusing to fight against the brother of his intended,
Clamydes declares everlasting friendship with his erstwhile
enemy. They proceed to the court of the King of Denmark,
where Clyomon is reunited to his family. Brian Sans Foy is
also at the court, still posing as Clamydes; but his cowardice
betrays him, and he is imprisoned. Clyomon is united with
Neronis, and Clamydes with Juliana.

Comments

Clyomon and Clamydes is a hybrid play very similar to
Common Conditions (No. VIII). Brian Sans Foy may well be

the best example in all English literature of a man who persistently admits his own cowardice. The usual punishing of the Vice at the end of the play is lacking here, as it is in *The Longer Thou Livest* (No. XXVI).

Critical Studies
Littleton, Betty J. *"Clyomon and Clamydes:* A Critical Edition." *DA,* 24:730-731 (1963).

VII. COBBLER'S PROPHESY, 1580-94
(Robert Wilson)

The Cobblers Prophesie. Written by Robert Wilson, Gent. John Danter for Cuthbert Burby, 1594.

Editions
W. Dibelius. *Jahrbuch,* XXXIII, 1914.
*A. C. Wood. *MSR,* 1914.

Dramatis Personae

Ceres	Codrus
Mercury	A Porter of Mars
Ralph Cobbler	A Herald
Zelota, his wife	Venus
Sateros, a soldier	Mars
Contempt, alias Content	Folly
A Country Gentleman	Newfangle
A Scholar	A Duke
Ennius, a courtier	Ru ⎫
Thalia ⎫	Ina ⎭ waiting maids to Venus
Clio ⎬ three Muses	A Messenger to the Duke
Melpomene ⎭	A Prisoner
Charon	A Priest

(Supernumeraries) Jupiter, Juno, Apollo, Bacchus, Vulcan, Diana, Niceness, Daliance, Jealousy, the infant Ruina, and the Duke's daughter.

Length of the play: 1,696 lines.

Plot Summary

In his role as messenger, Mercury summons Ceres to an emergency meeting of the gods. The cobbler Ralph is chosen to make known to the Boeotians the evils into which they have fallen in these times of apparent peace — insidious treachery from foreign enemies, false courtiers, decadent scholars, conservative and selfish country gentlemen. Literature is at a low ebb. The Muses Clio (History) and Melpomene (Tragedy) suffer from indolence, although Thalia (Comedy and Pastoral Poetry) manages to write a fairly inept pageant of Pleasure. Mars, the god of War, heedless of the Cobbler's warning, has also been infected by the noxious stagnation of peace. Dressed in silk, he falls asleep to the music of Folly, Niceness, Newfangle, Daliance, and Jealousy, and to the voice of Venus. When Mars learns that Venus has absconded with Contempt (alias Content), the Vice, he vows eternal hatred of Venus. The just Duke praises the soldier and listens to Ralph Cobbler's warning that the courtier Ennius seeks the nobleman's life. But Ralph's mad wife Zelota chases and stabs Ennius with his own dagger.

A final prophesy of war is delivered by Ralph and a messenger announces that foreign forces have landed and are overrunning Boeotia. Troups are marshaled and learn to defend the country. The Duke, the Scholar, and the Priest do penance by burning their sins along with the Cabin of Contempt. Shortly they receive news of victory. The Soldier and Scholar are reconciled, and Ralph learns that he and Zelota have been under a spell from Mercury all the while.

Comments

The *Cobbler's Prophesy* is a hybrid play whose subject is the health of the nation. Although the setting is given as Boeotia, the character of the play is entirely English: the enemy are the Spanish, the attacking force is an armada. Strong feeling is shown against the upper classes; the Duke, however, represents a minority of the nobility properly oriented.

Other "estates" plays:
> *King John* (No. XXII).
> *Looking Glass for London and England* (No. XXVII).
> *Play of the Weather* (No. LVI).
> *Satire of the Three Estates* (No. XLV).
> *Three Ladies of London* (No. XLVIII).
> *Three Lords and Three Ladies of London* (No. L).
> *Tide Tarrieth No Man* (No. LI).

Critical Studies

Lavin, J. A. "Two Notes on The *Cobbler's Prophesy.*" *N&Q,* 9:137-139 (1962).

Gatch, K. H. "Robert Wilson, Actor and Dramatist." Yale University Dissertation, 1928.

Mann, Irene. "The Dibelius Edition of *The Cobbler's Prophesie.*" *N&Q,* 189:48-50 (1945).

_____ "Notes on the Malone Society Reprint of *The Cobbler's Prophesy.*" *The Library,* 4th ser. 26:181-189 (1946).

_____ "A Political Cancel in *"The Coblers Prophesie."* *The Library,* 4th ser. 23:94-100 (1943).

_____ "The Text of the Plays of Robert Wilson." University of Virginia Dissertation, 1942.

Sisson, Sarah Trumbull. *"The Coblers Prophesie,* a Morality: Edited with Introduction and Notes." University of Illinois Dissertation, 1942.

VIII. COMMON CONDITIONS, c. 1576
(Anonymous)

An excellent and pleasant Comedie, termed after the name of the Vice, Common Conditions, drawne out of the most famous historie of Galiarbus Duke of Arabia, and of the good and euil successe of him and his two children, Sedmond his son, and Clarisia his daughter: Set forth with delectable mirth, and pleasant shewes. William How for John Hunter, n.d., but entered in the books of the Stationers' Company in 1576

Editions
Brandl (fragmentary text).
Farmer, 1908 (fragmentary text).
*C. F. Tucker Brooke. *Elizabethan Club Reprints.* New Haven, 1915.

Dramatis Personae
The Prologue
Galiarbus, the old duke of Arabia
Sedmond, his son
Clarisia, his daughter
Common Conditions, the Vice [Mediocrity]
Shift ⎫
Drift ⎬ three Tinkers
Unthrift ⎭
Metrea, a maid [Clarisia in disguise]
Leostines, a knight that loveth Metrea
Lamphedon, a knight that loveth Clarisia and fighteth for her
Nomides, a knight that loveth Metrea
Cardolus, a knight that fighteth with Lamphedon
M[aster] of the ship ⎫
Master's Mate ⎬ four Mariners
Boateswaine ⎪
Shipboy ⎭

25

> Mountagos, a Spaniard
> Sabia, his daughter
> Lomia, a natural fool
>> Six may play this Comedy.

Length of the play: 1,904 lines.

Plot Summary

Galiarbus, recently ordered into banishment by King Arbaccus of Arabia, takes leave of his son Sedmond and daughter Clarisia. They naturally wish to follow their father into exile, but he prevails upon them to remain at home. After the departure of Galiarbus, Sedmond suggests that he and Clarisia live in quiet retirement at home, but Clarisia vehemently upbraids her brother for such easy acquiescence in their father's exile. The Vice, Common Conditions, warns them that their return home will imperil their lives. Alone on stage, he boasts that it was he who caused Galiarbus to be falsely charged with treason. Now, afraid of exposure at court, he has persuaded the two young people also to flee so that he may have company. We learn that his real name is Mediocrity.

The three tinkers, Shift, Drift, and Unthrift, enter singing about their profession. Unthrift suggests that they waylay Sedmond, Clarisia, and Common Conditions as they flee from Arabia. Common Conditions ably demonstrates his cleverness when he outsmarts the three thieves and leaves with Clarisia for Phrygia. He promises that they will find there not only Galiarbus but also Sedmond who has just been lost.

Galiarbus has been made a lord in Phrygia, but sorrows at the loss of his two children. Lamphedon, son of the Duke of Phrygia, has seen and fallen in love with Clarisia. Knowing that Clarisia also loves Lamphedon, Common Conditions, under the alias of Affection, offers his assistance to the two lovers to gain their gratitude. Sabia, daughter of the Spanish Doctor Mountagos, meets the poor knight Nomides, with

26

whom she has fallen in love. Unfortunately for Sabia, Nomides, in reality the wandering Sedmond, scorns her affection.

The Duchess mother of Lamphedon becomes jealous of Clarisia, who, with Lamphedon, sets sail for Thrace expecting a generous welcome from her uncle King Mountaynio. Common Conditions in the meantime has become the leader of a band of pirates who both rob and separate the two lovers.

Doctor Mountagos coaxes from Sabia the name of her lover and plans to prepare a love potion to turn the attentions of Nomides to the lovelorn girl. Lamphedon confronts the pirates and learns from them that Clarisia is at the castle of Cardolus on the isle of Marofus. But, under the name of Metrea, she is in reality staying at the home of the knight Leostines while Common Conditions searches for Lamphedon at Marofus. Lamphedon comes to Marofus, subdues the tyrant Cardolus, and sets free all the women Cardolus has held captive.

Nomides has fallen in love with Metrea, but she scorns him just as he had rejected Sabia. Lamphedon is about to take his own life for grief for the lost Clarisia, but Common Conditions, thinking Lamphedon is Cardolus, stays his hand. Cleverly making the best of his mistake, Common Conditions accompanies Lamphedon to seek out Metrea, who is still a servant of Leostines. The two lovers are united, and Lamphedon is hidden in Clarisia's chamber. Common Conditions, using the alias Gravity, reports this information to Leostines, who apprehends Clarisia and Lamphedon and commands that they be poisoned for impurity and for plotting Leostine's murder. The play ends as they are about to drink the poison. The Epilogue explains that lack of time forbids the completion of the action, and prays for God's blessing on Queen Elizabeth and on all the people.

Comments

Common Conditions, a hybrid play, is related in plot and

in its prologue to *Clyomon and Clamydes* (No. VI). The speech of Doctor Mountagos is an early example of broken English on the stage. The play undoubtedly was meant to have a happy ending, but the Prologue warns us not to judge in advance. The confession of the playwright that he could not bring his piece within the practicable time limit is unique in the morality drama.

Critical Studies
Brooke, C. K. Tucker. "On the Source of *Common Conditions.*" *MLN,* 31:474-478 (1916).

IX. CONFLICT OF CONSCIENCE, 1575-81
(Nathaniel Woodes)

First issue: *An excellent new Commedie, Intituled: The Conflict of Conscience. Contayning, The most lamentable Hystorie, of the desperation of Frauncis Spera, who forsooke the truth of Gods Gospell, for feare of the losse of life and wordly goodes.* Compiled, by Nathaniell Woodes. Minister, in Norwich. Richard Bradocke, 1581.

Second Issue: *An excellent new Commedie, Intituled: The Conflict of Conscience. Contayninge, A most lamentable example of the dolefull desperation of a miserable worldlinge, termed, by the name of Philologus, who forsooke the truth of Gods Gospell, for feare of the losse of lyfe, & wordly goods.* Compiled, by Nathaniell Woodes. Minister, in Norwich. Richard Bradocke, 1581.

28

Editions
J. P. Collier. *Five Old Plays.* London: Roxburghe Club, 1851.
  (combines title page of first issue with text of second).
Dodsley, VI.
*Herbert Davis and F. P. Wilson. *MRS,* 1952.

Dramatis Personae
  The Actors names divided into six parts, most convenient
  for such as be disposed, either to shew this Comedy in
  private houses, or otherwise.

Prologue Mathetes Conscience Paphinitius	for one	Satan Tyranny Spirit Horror	for one
Hypocrisy Theologus	for one	Eusevius Avarice	
Cardinal Caconus	for one	Suggestion Gisbertus	for one
Philologus	for one	Nuntius	

Length of the play: 2,494 lines.

Plot Summary
  The Prologue reveals the play to be taken from the life of
Francis Spira, who will be known as Philologus. In the action
proper, Satan first delivers a monologue in which he boasts of
former triumphs and then declares the Pope to be his eldest
child, to whom Avarice and Tyranny have been given as pro-
tectors. Philologus and his friend Mathetes converse on godly
matters — the nature of the true Church, the tribulations of
the just, the saving nature of affliction — all supported by
examples from Scripture. Hypocrisy, Avarice, and Tyranny
argue at some length which of them will be leader. They
unite, however, in the common purpose of advancing the
Pope and the legates his ministers, and thus in deluding the
laity. Tyranny and Avarice adopt new names, Zeal and

Careful Provision, and don corresponding disguises. To the dismay of righteous Philologus, their efforts to bring Popish ways back into the land succeed. The ignorant priest Caconus informs on Philologus to the three vices. Apprehended, Philologus skillfully denies both the authority of the Pope and the real presence of Christ in the Blessed Sacrament. For these views, he is condemned to prison, where Sensual Suggestion, a servant of Hypocrisy, persuades him to recant. Both Spirit and Conscience attempt to confirm Philologus in Protestantism; but the arguments of Sensual Suggestion prevail, and Philologus returns to the Catholic Church. Having lived for some time as a prosperous Catholic, Philologus is visited by Horror, who easily brings his victim to despair. The efforts of two friends, Eusebius and Theologus, to move Philologus to repentance are in vain. Unable even to pray, he gives himself up to damnation and takes his own life.

(A second issue of this play differs from the first in the Prologue, which omits Francis Spira's name; the name is also left out of the title page and in the sixth and final act. Here the Nuntius announces not the tragic suicide of Philologus but his conversion and death in God.)

Comments

The Conflict of Conscience, a Protestant play, is the only English morality taken from the life of a real person, Francis Spira. The play is primarily concerned with the backsliding of Protestants to Catholicism.

Other Protestant plays:
> *King Darius* (No. XXI).
> *King John* (No. XXII).
> *New Custom* (No. XL).
> *Three Laws* (No. XLIX).

See Coming of Death (Appendix I).
> The Devil in the Moralities (Appendix IV).

Critical Studies

Cambell, Lily Bess. "Doctor Faustus: A Case of Conscience."
 PMLA, 67:219-239 (1952).
Jackson, William. "Woodes' *Conflict of Conscience.*" *TLS,*
 Sept. 7, 1933, p. 592.
Oliver, Leslie. "John Foxe and *The Conflict of Conscience.*"
 RES, 25:1-9 (1949).
Wine, Celesta. "Nathaniel Wood in *The Conflict of Con-*
 science." University of Chicago Dissertation, 1934.
_____ "Nathaniel Woodes, Author of the Morality Play
 The Conflict of Conscience." *RES,* 15:458-463 (1939).
_____ "Nathaniel Wood's *Conflict of Conscience.*"
 PMLA, 50:661-678 (1935).
_____ "Woode's *Conflict of Conscience.*" *TLS,* Nov. 23,
 1933, p. 840.

X. CRUEL DEBTOR, c. 1565
(Lewis Wager or W. Wager)

A ballett intituled an Interlude of the Cruel Debtor, by
Wager. Thomas Colwell, 1565. Only four leaves which are a
composite of two fragments survive.

Editions

F. J. Furnivall. *New Shakespeare Society's Transactions,*
 1877-79 (reprints three leaves).
*W. W. Greg. *Malone Society Collections,* I(1911) and II
 (1923).

Dramatis Personae

Flattery	Basileus
Rigor	Proniticus
Simulation	
Ophiletis	

Length of the fragment: 265 lines.

Plot Summary

Flattery and Rigor plan to play a trick on Simulation as payment in kind for all his pranks at their expense. They will pretend to fight, and when Simulation attempts to break them up, they will both turn on him and give him a good beating. The plan works well, but Simulation finally discovers the joke and promises to repay them one day. From this point the plot follows that of the gospel parable of the unforgiving servant. Ophiletis, the servant who has squandered the King's money, is called before King Basileus by the steward Proniticus. The fragment ends with a plea for mercy by Ophiletis.

Comments

The Cruel Debtor is a gospel play based on Matthew xviii, 22-35.

XI. ENOUGH IS AS GOOD AS A FEAST, 1560-69
(W. Wager)

A Comedy or Enterlude intituled, Inough is as good as a feast, very fruteful, godly and ful of pleasant mirth. Compiled by W. Wager. John Allde, n.d.

Editions
S. de Ricci. *Huntington Facsimile Reprints.* New York, 1920.
*R. Mark Benbow. *Regents Renaissance Drama Series.*
(University of Nebraska) Lincoln, Neb., 1967.

Dramatis Personae

Seven may easily play this interlude

Worldly Man } for one   Inconsideration ⎫
Prologue   ⎫   Servant   ⎪
Heavenly Man ⎬ for one   Rest   ⎬ for one
Contentation ⎫   Prophet   ⎪
Temerity   ⎪   Precipitation ⎫
Ignorance   ⎬ for one   Tenant   ⎬ for one
Satan   ⎪   God's Plague   ⎪
Enough } for one   Physician
Hireling }   Covetise the Vice for another

(Ignorance is also referred to as Sir Nicholas and the
Physician as Master Flebeshiten.)

Length of the play: 1,541 lines.

Plot Summary
Responsive to the admonitions of his virtuous counterpart
Heavenly Man, Worldly Man renounces his attachment to
riches and is converted. (From this point until the very end,
the play concerns itself exclusively with the career of Wordly
Man, the wayward member of the bifurcated Mankind figure.)
While Enough is assigned as mentor to Worldly Man,
Temerity, Precipitation, and Inconsideration bring their
leader, Covetise, news of Worldly Man's conversion to virtue.
Promising to take immediate action before God's grace can
take hold, Covetise orders his gown, cap, and chain to be
brought to him and gives his assistants new names — Reason
(Inconsideration), Agility (Temerity), Ready Wit (Precipitation). Their plan of action is next decided upon. Temerity
will first gain favor with Worldly Man, next Precipitation will

cause him to act and think rashly, then Inconsideration will
disgrace Enough. They will have thus prepared the way for
Covetise (alias Policy) to effect the final relapse of the sinner.

Having secured a word with his victim alone, Covetise, by
means of moans and tears, skillfully convinces Worldly Man
of his sincere love and solicitude. In spite of the arguments of
Enough, Worldly Man slowly but surely falls prey to the
vices. They declare themselves to be Policy and Ready Wit,
old friends of his father, and promise also to double Worldly
Man's riches. The unpaid hireling and the rent burdened
Tenant who beg Covetise to intercede for them with their
master Worldly Man reveal his ruthless business tactics.
Worldly Man has no intention of gratifying his suitors and is
even planning another conquest in real estate when the voice
of the Prophet warns of impending death. Worldly Man is
thereupon stricken by God's plague, and the Physician Master
Flebeshiten is called in to analyse the illness. Worldly Man
dies as he dictates the first words of his will. Rejoicing at still
another human conquest, Satan carries Worldly Man to hell.
Enough, Contentation, and Rest congratulate Heavenly Man
on his perseverance in virtue, and, once more, point out the
moral implicit in the play's title.

Comments

Like *The Longer Thou Livest* (No. XXVI), *Enough is as
Good as a Feast* is a Protestant (Calvinist) morality. The dis-
tinction between those elected for salvation and those
destined for damnation is clearly dramatized in the bifurcated
Mankind figures of Worldly Man and Heavenly Man.

Other plays with a bifurcated Mankind figure:
> *Glass of Government* (No. XIII).
> *Like Will to Like* (No. XXV).
> *Nice Wanton* (No. XLI).
> *Tide Tarrieth No Man* (No. LI).
> *Trial of Treasure* (No. LIII).

See The Devil in the Moralities (Appendix IV).

XII. EVERYMAN, 1480-1500
(Anonymous)

*Here begynneth a treatise how the hye fader of heuen send-
eth dethe to somon euery creature to come and gyue a
counte of theyr lyues in this worlde, and is in maner of a
morall playe.* John Skot, n.d. Fragments of two earlier versions exist. Both are by Pynson and lack dates and title pages.

Editions
(The following are the principal early editions of *Everyman*
and a few of the modern editions.)
T. Hawkins. *Origin of the English Drama,* I. London, 1773.
H. Logeman. Ghent, 1892 (this edition includes the Dutch
play *Elckerlijk*).
A. W. Pollard. *Fifteenth Century Prose and Verse.* London,
1903.
W. W. Greg. *Materialien,* IV, 1904 (First Skot edition).
*Farmer, 1905.
W. W. Greg. *Materialien,* XXIV (Second Skot edition).
A. T. Quiller-Couch. *Select English Classics.* London, 1909.
Ernest Rhys. *Everman's Library,* 1909.
W. W. Greg. *Materialien,* XXVIII, 1910. (Both Pynson
fragments).
Adams.
A. W. Pollard. *English Miracle Plays, Moralities and Inter-
ludes.* Oxford, 1927.
J. B. Hubbell and J. O. Beaty. *An Introduction to Drama.*
New York 1927.
A. C. Cawley. Manchester: University of Manchester Press,
1961.

Dramatis Personae

Messenger	Knowledge
God	Confession
Death	Beauty

Everyman	Strength
Fellowship	Discretion
Kindred	Five Wits
Goods	Angel
Good Deeds	Doctor

Length of the play: 921 lines.

Plot Summary

The Messenger introduces both the subject of the play, the Summoning of Everyman, and then God the Father who declares his anger at the traitorous behavior of mankind. God, therefore, bids his messenger Death to summon men to an accounting. Seeing Everyman nearby, Death accosts him with the grim news of impending judgement. Having realized the full impact of the summons of Death, Everyman tries to bribe the unwelcome messenger with £1000, but then learns that Death is a respecter of neither wealth nor individuals. Everyone must die in his turn. Other typically medieval views of death are expounded before Everyman is allowed to search for any friends who will accompany him to God's judgement seat. He first encounters Fellowship, who promises complete loyalty to Everyman, but then refuses to accompany his friend even one step once the true nature of Everyman's request is known. He next seeks out Kinsmen who, after promising fidelity, desert the moribund Everyman in his need. Despairing of his friends and relatives, Everyman next calls on his Goods and Riches, but learns that they are only of this world and have, in fact, brought many to Hell. Although unable to accompany Everyman because of weakness, Good Deeds, nonetheless, offers his sister knowledge to help make the aweful reckoning. Knowledge leads Everyman to Confession and, once the penance is fulfilled, Everyman rejoins Good Deeds now liberated from the weight of Everyman's sins. Overjoyed in his newfound forgiveness, Everyman vests himself with the garment of contrition and completes his reckoning. Accompanying Everyman on his journey will be his mental and physical faculties: Discretion, Strength, Beauty, and his Five Wits. Comforted for the ordeal ahead, Everyman makes a charitable will and prepares to receive Holy Communion. While he is receiving the Sacrament and also Extreme Unction, Knowledge and the Five Wits discourse on the greatness and necessity of the priesthood. They, however, desert him. Left alone with Good Deeds, Everyman dies. An Angel welcomes him to paradise and a Doctor ends the play with a salutary exhortation to the audience.

Comments

Everyman is the most famous of all the English moralities. Like *Pride of Life* (No. XLIII), *Everyman* is exclusively concerned with approaching Death.

See Coming of Death (Appendix I).

Critical Studies

Adolf, Helen. "From *Everyman* and *Eleckerlÿc* to Hofmannsthal and Kafka." *CL,* 9:204-214 (1957).

Bang, W. "Zu Everyman." *Eng St,* 35:444-449 (1905).

Conley, John. "The Doctirne of Friendship in *Everyman.*" *Speculum,* 44:374-382 (1969).

_____ "The Reference to Judas Maccabeus in *Everyman.*" *N&Q,* 14:50-51 (1967).

Fifield, Merle. *The Castle in the Circle.* Ball State Monograph 6. Muncie, Ind.: Ball State University Press, 1967. [Staging of *Pride of Life* (No. XLIII), *Wisdom Who is Christ* (No. LVII), *Mankind* (No. XXXII), and *Everyman.*]

Green, J. T. "Criticism of *Everyman.*" *ILN,* 186:592 (1935).

Holthausen, Ferdinand. "Zu *Everyman.*" *AngBbl,* 32:212-215 (1921).

_____ "Zu *Everyman.*" *Archiv,* 92:411-412 (1894).

Holthausen, Ferdinand and E. Kolbing. "Zu *Everyman.*" *EngSt,* 21:449-450 (1895).

James, S. B. *"Everyman."* *Mag,* 46:222-225 (1930).

Johnson, Wallace H. "The Double Desertion of *Everyman."* *AN&Q,* 6:85-87 (1968).

Kaula, David. "Time and the Timeless in *Everyman* and *Dr. Faustus." CE,* 22:9-14 (1960).

Kossman, H. "Felawship His Fer: A Note on Everyman's False Friend." *ES,* 45:Supplement, 157-160 (1964).

Manly, J. M. *"Elckerlÿc-Everyman:* the Question of Priority." *MP,* 8:269-277 (1910).

Roersch, A. *"Elckerlÿc-Everyman-Homulus-Hekastus." Archiv,* 113:13-16 (1904).

Ryan, Lawrence, V. "Doctrine and Dramatic Structure in *Everyman." Speculum,* 32:722-735 (1957).

Takahashi, Genji. *A Study of Everyman.* Tokyo: Ai-iku-sha, n.d.

Thomas, Helen S. "The Meaning of the Character Knowledge in *Everyman." MQ,* 14:3-13 (1961).

_____ "Some Analogues of *Everyman." MQ,* 16:97-103 (1963).

Thaler, A. "Shakespeare, Daniel, and *Everyman." PQ,* 15:217-218 (1936).

Tigg, E. R. "Is *Elckerlÿc* Prior to *Everyman?" JEGP,* 38:568-596 (1939).

Van Laam, Thomas F. *"Everyman:* A Structural Analysis." *PMLA,* 78:465-475 (1963).

Vocht, Henry de. *Everyman: A Comparative Study of Texts and Sources.* Louvain: Librairie Universitaire, 1947.

Vos, R. *"Elckerlÿc-Everyman-Homulus-Der Sünden loin ist des toid." TNTL,* 82:129-143 (1966).

Wood, Francis A. *"Elckerlÿc-Everyman:* the Question of Priority." *MP,* 8:279-302 (1910).

Young, S. "Production of *Everyman." NR,* 53:164-165 (1927).

Zandvoort, R. W. *"Elckerlÿc-Everyman." ES,* 23:1-9 (1941).

XIII. GLASS OF GOVERNMENT, 1575
(George Gascoigne)

A tragicall Comedie so entituled, bycause therin are handled aswell the rewardes for Vertues, as also the punishment for Vices. Done by George Gascoigne Esquier. C. Barker, 1575.

Edition
John W. Cunliffe. *The Complete Works of George Gascoigne.* Cambridge, 1910. (Reprinted, Grosse Pointe, Michigan: The Scholarly Press, 1969.

Dramatis Personae

Phylopaes and Phylocalus	Two parents being near neighbors
Gnomaticus	a Schoolmaster
Phylautus Phylomusus	Sons to Phylopaes
Phylosarchus Phylotimus	Sons to Phylocalus
Severus	the Margrave
Echo	the Parasite
Lamia	the Harlot
Pandarina	Aunt to Lamia
Dick Drumme	the Roister
Nuntii,	two Messengers
Onaticus	servant to the Schoolmaster
Fidus	servant to Phylopaes
Ambidexter	servant to Phylocalus
Chorus	four grave Burghers

The Comedy to be presented as it were in Antwerp.

Length of the play: approximately 3,200 lines.

Plot Summary
Set in Antwerp, the play opens with the conversation of

Phylopaes and Phylocalus concerning their sons. They each
have two sons who have been brought up together and now,
at the ages of twenty and nineteen years, are about ready to
enter a university. Before sending the boys off, the fathers
think it wise to entrust them to some honest schoolmaster to
learn their duties to God, to their Prince, to their parents, to
their country, and to themselves. The loyal servant Fidus re-
spectfully suggests as tutor a pious schoolmaster named
Gnomaticus who is at the present time unemployed. Although Gnomaticus modestly refuses to fix his salary, he
agrees to instruct the boys. They are brought in and
Phylocalus introduces his sons Phylosarchus and Phylotimus,
and Phylopaes likewise presents his two sons Phylautus and
Phylomusus. All four boys show themselves polite and
obedient and willingly put themselves into the care of
Gnomaticus. The first lesson begins immediately. Gnomaticus
discovers that the boys have read Erasmus' *Colloquia.*
Cicero's *DeOfficiis* and *Epistolae,* and some Vergil. His plan
is to instruct them in four main points: God and his ministers, the King and his officers, the duties toward their
country and the elders, and duties toward parents and toward
themselves. Before dinner, Gnomaticus preaches to them on
the first chapter emphasizing the fear, love and trust of God,
and the reverence and love due his ministers.

The setting changes to the street where the harlot Lamia
complains that her profession is lately hindered by prying
ministers. Her aunt Pandarina gives her three rules to live by
while a prostitute: trust no man, refuse no man if he has
money, and love no man when he ceases to give gifts "since
lyberall gifts are the glewe of everlasting love." Echo, the
Parasite, suggests that they ensnare the four boys and the
group moves to Pandarina's house to formulate plans in
secret.

Next follow more lessons from Gnomaticus — the honor,
obedience, and love of kings; the thanks, defense, and profit
owed one's country; the reverence, love, and defnese of the

elders; and the honor, love, and relief of parents. Left to themselves, Phylautus and Phylosarchus voice their dissatisfaction with the trite teaching of Gnomaticus and resolve to attend the University of Douai. The younger boys, Phylomusus and Phylotimus, remain humbly receptive to their teachers godly instruction.

Echo now easily causes the two older boys to become enamored of Lamia, and, setting up the pretext that the Margrave desires to see them, brings Phylautus and Phylosarchus to a rendez-vous with her. The meeting takes place as planned, but someone informs on the boys to their fathers who then resolve to send them away from Antwerp to the University of Douai. Meanwhile, the younger sons have been intent on their homework and recite to each other their own poems on the duties of a Christian to God, country, and themselves.

When Phylopaes and Phylocalus learn that the two older boys have spent their time writing love sonnets and military poems, they decide to send them to Douai without delay. Phylautus and Phylosarchus of course do not want to leave Echo and Lamia, and had even planned a dinner for that same evening. They are, however, sent off and Echo, Lamia, and Pandarina are arrested for corrupting youth. Only Dick Drumme, one of Lamia's group, has escaped arrest and he announces his intentions of following the boys to Douai.

Time passes and a messenger brings letters from Douai by which the parents learn that Phylautus and Phylosarchus are wasting their time in brothels waiting to be joined by Lamia and Echo. The news is not all bad because Phylotimus has been chosen secretary to the Palsgrave and Phylomusus is to be a preacher in Geneva. The parents send Fidus to apprehend Ambidexter, Phylocalus' servant, who has helped to corrupt the boys. Without certain proof of the guilt of Echo, Lamia, and Pandarina, Margrave Severus admits he must free them. But when he learns that Echo impersonated one of his own staff, Severus has him whipped and Lamia and Pandarina

41

set on the cucking stool. All are then banished. Fidus arrives from the Palsgrave's court with Ambidexter and announces that Phylautus and Dick Drumme were hanged for robbery and that Phylosarchus is almost dead from being whipped three times for fornication in Geneva. The play ends as Gnomaticus accompanies Fidus to the boys' parents with the sad news.

Comments

The *Glass of Government* is a "youth" play in direct imitation of the educational plays of the Low Lands. The Mankind figures are here four: Phylautus and Phylosarchus follow the road to perdition and Phylomusus and Phylotimus that of virtue.

Other "youth" plays:
> *Hickscorner* (No. XVI).
> *Lusty Juventus* (No. XXX).
> *Marriage of Wit and Wisdom* (No. XXXIV).
> *Misogonus* (No. XXXVI).
> *Nice Wanton* (No. XLI).
> *Wit and Science* (No. LVIII).
> *Youth* (No. LIX).

Other plays with a bifurcated Mankind figure:
> *Enough is as Good as a Feast* (No. XI).
> *Like Will to Like* (No. XXV).
> *Nice Wanton* (No. XLI).
> *Tide Tarrieth No Man* (No. LI).
> *Trial of Treasure* (No. LIII).

Critical Studies

Feldman, Abraham Bronson. "Dutch Humanism and the Tudor Dramatic Tradition." *N&Q*, 197:357-360 (1962).

Herford, C. H. *"Glasse of Government."* *EngSt*, 9:201-209 (1886).

Price, John E. "A Secondary Bibliography of George Gascoigne with an Introduction Summarizing the Trend of Gascoigne Scholarship." *BB*, 25:138-140 (1968).

Prouty, C. T. *George Gascoigne, Elizabethan Courtier, Soldier and Poet.* New York: Columbia University Press, 1942.

Tannenbaum, Samuel A. *George Gascoigne, A Concise Bibliography.* Elizabethan Bibliographies No. 26. New York: Samuel A. Tannenbaum, 1942.

XIV. GODLY QUEEN HESTER, 1525-29
(Anonymous)

A newe enterlude drawen oute of the holy scripture of godly queene Hester, verye necessary newly made and imprinted, this present yere. M.D.L.X.I. William Pickering and Thomas Hacket.

Editions
J. P. Collier. *Illustrations of Early English Popular Literature,* I. London, 1863.
A. B. Grosart. *Miscellanies of The Fuller Worthies' Library,* IV. London, 1873.
W. W. Greg. *Materialien,* V (1904).
*Farmer, 1906.

Dramatis Personae

The Prologue	Pride
King Assuerus	Adulation
Three Gentlemen	Ambition
Hamon	Hardy Dardy
Mardocheus	A Jew
Hester	Arbona
Pursuivant	Scriba

(Needed also are a group of choristers who sing when Hester prays for her people and maidens from whom King Assuerus chooses Hester.)

Length of the play: 1,180 lines.

Plot Summary

Godly Queen Hester begins with a debate at the court of King Assuerus on the subject of the relative merits of riches, noble birth, and virtue. King Assuerus and his council agree not only that virtue is the most to be desired but also that Justice is the virtue par excellence of a king. When Assuerus informs the council of his intentions to wed, the play proceeds according to the traditional Biblical story. Hester is chosen among all the women presented for the King's inspection. It is the sixteenth century adapter's great insistence on the virtues of Hester that renders evident the homiletic purpose of the play. Hester is

> . . . . a virgin pure
> A pearl undefiled and of conscience clear,
> Sober, sad, gentle, meek, and demure;
> In learning and literature profoundly seen,
> In wisdom eke semblant to Saba the Queen.

Once the new Queen has retired, Pride, Adulation, and Ambition speak lines of choral commentary leaving no doubt as to the moral depravity of the King's adviser, Hamon. Pride complains that Hamon has as many gowns as he. Adulation and Ambition add other charges, some of which have little to do with the Hester story. The vices all agree that they are out-viced by Hamon and bequeath him their pride, subtlety, and ambition.

The Hester story resumes with the plot of Hamon to kill all Jews in the kingdom. Hester learns of this, and, at a banquet, intercedes for her people before Assuerus. Hamon is hanged on the gallows which he had prepared for Hester's uncle Mardocheus. Hester is given Hamon's estate to dispose as she sees fit. The play ends with public praise for Hester and her people.

Comments

Godly Queen Hester is a hybrid "vir ue" play emphasizing the virtues of Wisdom and Chastity. The charges of Pride, Adulation, and Ambition against Hamon are clearly topical in nature and concern Cardinal Wolsey. Similarly, the situation in which Hester finds herself is analogous to that of Queen Katherine of Aragon. Pride, Adulation, and Ambition are purely choric, homiletic figures. Hardy Dardy is a natural fool.

Other "virtue" plays:
Appius and Virginia (No. III).
Life and Repentance of Mary Magdalene (No. XXIV).
Patient and Meek Grissell (No. XLII).
Virtuous and Godly Susanna (No. LIV).

Critical Studies

Blackburn, Ruth Harriett. "Tudor Biblical Drama." *DA,* 17:1746-1747 (1957).
Roston, Murray. *Biblical Drama in England from the Middle Ages to the Present Day.* London: Faber and Faber, 1968.

XV. GOOD ORDER, 1500-33
(John Skelton)

Only the last 131 lines of this play and Rastell's colophon survive.

Edition

G. L. Frost and R. Nash. *SP,* 41:483-491 (1944).

XV

Dramatis Personae
  Good Order
  Old Christmas
  Riot
  Gluttony
  Prayer
  [Abstinence — possible speaker of lines condemning
          Gluttony]

Length of the fragment: 131 lines.

Plot Summary
  Riot and Gluttony are brought in by Good Order before
Old Christmas on charges of rebellion. On the recommenda-
tion of Good Order, Old Christmas banishes the traitors.
They decide to seek out the New World and ask for spending
money, but are refused. Lines condemning Gluttony and
praising Abstinence are spoken by an unnamed character,
possibly Abstinence. The fragment ends with lines defining
prayer by a character of that name.

Comments
  There is no real reason to doubt the authority of Bale that
the author of *Good Order* is Skelton. If the rebellion scene
was enacted in the first section now lost, *Good Order* would
have contained yet another example of the military
Psychomachia.
  See *Psychomachia* (Appendix V).

XVI. HICKSCORNER, 1513-16
(Anonymous)

The interlude of Hycke scorner. Wynken de Worde, n.d.

Editions
T. Hawkins. *Origin of the English Drama,* I. London, 1733.
Dodsley, I.
Manly, I.
*Farmer, 1905.

Dramatis Personae

Pity	Contemplation
Perseverance	Freewill
Imagination	Hickscorner

Length of the play: 1,026 lines.

Plot Summary
The two virtues, Pity and Contemplation, begin the play in a dialogue concerning their activities at Christ's passion. Perseverance, the good friend and kinsman of Contemplation, joins them for a discussion of two prevalent social evils of the late Middle Ages: first, the great extent of poverty and the accompanying suppression of the poor by the rich; second, the worldliness of the clergy. At their departure, the action turns to Freewill and Imagination, two minor vices, who narrate their exploits in the stews. They then introduce the Vice, Hickscorner, who delivers an entertaining account of his recent voyages throughout the world. They agree to go wenching that same night, but fall to fighting when Freewill insults the parents of Imagination. Pity tries to convert the vices, but is clapped in irons and left to suffer patiently while they go to their revels. Contemplation and Perseverance find Pity in the stocks and unloose him offering proper commendations for his great kindness toward his oppressors. Perseverance and

XVI

Contemplation remonstrate with Freewill; after much argument they convert him and his companion Imagination. It is decided that Freewill hereafter dwell with Contemplation, and Imagination (now called Good Remembrance) will attend on Perseverance. Perseverance speaks the closing lines of exhortation to virtue to the audience.

Comments

Hickscorner is an early example of popular theater. Freewill and Imagination, the Henrican survivals of the earlier Mankind, are abstractions in name only. Examples of both the military and verbal Psychomachia are found in *Hickscorner*. The humiliation of a virtuous character in the stocks was to become a popular feature in the plots of many later plays. See *Mankind* (No. XXXII), *Mundus et Infans* (No. XXXVII), and *Youth* (No. LIX) for three other moralities concerned with disrespectful youth.

Other "youth" plays:

> *Glass of Government* (No. XIII).
> *Lusty Juventus* (No. XXX).
> *Marriage of Wit and Wisdom* (No. XXXIV).
> *Misogonus* (No. XXXVI).
> *Nice Wanton* (No. XLI).
> *Wit and Science,* (No. LVIII).

See Debate of the Heavenly Graces (Appendix III).
> *Psychomachia* (Appendix V).

Critical Studies

Greg, W. W. "Notes on Some Early Plays: *Hycke Scorner,* Reconstruction of a Treveris Edition, Known only from Two Leaves." *The Library,* Ser.4, 11:44-56 (1930).

Lancashire, Ian. "The Sources of *Hyckescorner." RES,* n.s. 22:257-273 (1971).

Schell, E. T. *"Youth* and *Hyckescorner:* Which Came First?" *PQ,* 45:468-474 (1966).

XVII. HORESTES, c. 1567
(John Pikering)

A Newe Enterlude of Vice Conteyninge, the Historye of Horestes, with the cruell reuengment of his Fathers death, vpon his one naturall Mother. By John Pikering. William Griffith, 1567.

Editions
J. P. Collier. *Illustrations of Old English Literature,* II. London, 1886.
Brandl.
*Daniel Seltzer. *MSR,* 1962.

Dramatis Personae
(The title page lists the players' names in columns and again divided for doubling. Only the doubling list is reproduced below.)
1. The Vice, Nature, and Duty
2. Rusticus, Idumeus, Second Soldier, Menelaus, and Nobles
3. Hodge, Counsel, Messenger, Nestor, and Commons
4. Horestes, a Woman, and Prologue
5. Haltersick, [First] Soldier, Egistus, Herald, Fame, Truth, and Idumeus
6. Hempstring, Clytemnestra, Provision, and Hermione.
(Needed also are two stage armies. It is not necessary that the part of Idumeus (2 and 5 above) be taken by two actors.)

Length of the play: 1,416 lines.

Plot Summary
The two rustics Hodge and Rusticus meet with the Vice, Revenge, who, faithful to his deceitful nature, sets the two men to quarreling and runs out giving each of them a good

smack. Horestes then enters, undecided whether to avenge his father's death. The decision is doubly difficult because it was his own mother Clytemnestra who murdered his father King Agamemnon to marry her lover Egistus. Dame Nature has advised Horestes that to kill one's mother is unnatural and counsels pity and forgiveness. On the other hand, filial duty demands that the monstrous crime be revenged. When Horestes prays to the gods for aid, the Vice, Revenge, poses as their messenger and extends divine approval for killing Clytemnestra and Egistus. Similar indorsement also comes from King Idumeus and his council who not only approve the revenge, but also equip Horestes with auxiliary troops. After the two soldiers Haltersick and Hempstring and the Vice, Revenge, have provided some comic relief, Nature again opts for forebearance, and Idumeus again recommends action.

A messenger interrupts the marital bliss of Clytemnestra and Egistus to announce that Horestes is at hand. They refuse to surrender their city and the armed conflict ensues. Taken in battle, Clytemnestra prays Horestes for her life and is held until after the death of Egistus in battle. In spite of a moment's hesitation, Horestes takes the life of his mother Clytemnestra. Fame announces that she must hereafter spread the news of the terrible deed and, thereby, cause Horestes eternal shame.

The business of revenge continues and Horestes now becomes its target. His maternal uncle Menelaus, desiring satisfaction for Clytemnestra's death, seeks to kill Horestes. King Idumeus and King Nestor convince Menelaus that Horestes was justified in his actions. A complete family and social reconciliation is brought about when Horestes marries Hermione, the daughter of Menelaus. Duty and Truth end the play in a manner typical of most Tudor moralities. Extending the obvious message of the play from the personal level to include also broader social applications, they maintain that none of the deaths would have occurred had the kingdom first been free of faction and dissension.

Comments

Horestes is a hybrid play and the first of a long series of English plays whose subject is revenge. The text of the play itself is noteworthy for its numerous stage directions. The Vice, not necessary for the Horestes plot, performs the role of chorus in most of his speaking lines.

Critical Studies

Brie, F. *"Horestes* von John Pikeryng." *EngSt,* 46:66-72 (1912).
de Chickera, E. B. "Horestes' Revenge — Another Interpretation." *N&Q,* 6:190 (1959).
Happé, P. "Tragic Themes in Three Tudor Moralities." *SEL,* 5:207-227 (1965). [Discussion of *Cambises* (No. IV), *Horestes,* and *Appius and Virginia* (No. III).]
Phillips, J. E. "A Revaluation of *Horestes."* *HLQ,* 18:227-244 (1955).

XVIII. IMPATIENT POVERTY, 1547-58
(Anonymous)

A newe Interlude of Impacyente pouerte newlye Imprinted. M.D.L.X. John King.

Editions
*Farmer, 1907.
H. B. McKerrow. *Materialien,* XXXIII (1911).

Dramatis Personae

Four men may well and easily play this Interlude

Peace ⎫
Colhazard ⎬ for one man
Conscience ⎭

Abundance ⎫
Misrule ⎬ for one man

Impatient Poverty ⎫
Prosperity ⎬ for one man
Poverty ⎭

Envy ⎫
Summoner ⎬ for one man

Length of the play: approximately 1,100 lines.

Plot Summary

The play begins with a debate on the subject of whether the national economy prospers more in times of peace than in times of war. Peace maintains that riches and prosperity come only when war and strife are lacking. Envy argues that war supports a good segment of society — soldiers, fabricators of weapons, doctors. The thoroughly sour-dispositioned Impatient Poverty for a time boldly scorns the reformative attempts of Peace, but suddenly converts and assumes the new name and dress of Prosperity. Conscience next tries to convert the usurer Abundance, who is willing to make any act of penance except that of restitution to those whom he has wronged. Using the alias of Charity, Envy persuades Conscience to flee the country in fear of his life because of the rampant corruption in Church, state, and even among the Commons. Still posing as Charity, Envy ingratiates himself with Prosperity and then plots with Misrule for his downfall. Prosperity is easily persuaded to enjoy the pleasure of cards, dice, and women to the dismay of Peace, who is forced bodily out of the place. With the help of the cardsharp Colhazard, Envy and Misrule so victimize Prosperity that he loses all his money, becomes Poverty once again, and is called by the Summoner to court. Abundance is also hailed before the magistrate to answer a charge of adultery, but he bribes the judge and goes free. Poverty, however, must suffer the punishments received because he has no money for bribery. Peace once again effects a conversion of Poverty and invests him with a new robe symbolic of his reformed state.

Comments

Impatient Poverty is a social, pro-Catholic play of Mary's reign.

Other "social" plays:

    Albion Knight (No. I).
    All for Money (No. II).
    Liberality and Prodigality (No. XXIII).
    Like Will to Like (No. XXV).
    Wealth and Health (No. LV).

See *Respublica* (No. XLIV).

    Temperance and Humility (No. XLVII).

    Also, *Cobbler's Prophesy* (No. VII) for a list of the "estates" plays, all of which are social pieces.

XIX. JACK JUGGLER, 1553-58
(Anonymous)

A new Enterlude for Chyldren to playe named Iacke Iugeler, both wytte, very playsent and merye, Neuer before Imprented. William Copland, n.d.

XIX

Editions
J. Haslewood. Roxburghe Club. London, 1820.
F. J. Child. *Four Old Plays.* Cambridge, Mass., 1848.
A. B. Grosart. *Miscellanies of The Fuller Worthies' Library,*
    IV. London, 1873.
Dodsley, IV.
E. W. Ashbee. *Dramatic Facsimiles.* London, 1876.
*Farmer, 1906.
E. L. Smart and W. W. Greg. *MSR,* 1933.
B. I. Evans and W. W. Greg, *MSR,* 1937.
M. Hussey and S. Agarwala. *The Play of the Weather by John
    Heywood and Other Tudor Comedies Adapted into
    Modern English.* New York: Theatre Arts, 1968.

Dramatis Personae
    Master Bongrace, a Gallant
    Dame Coy, his wife, a Gentlewoman
    Jack Juggler, the Vice
    Jenkin Careaway, a Lackey
    Alison Trip-and-Go, a Maid

Length of the play: approximately 1,100 lines.

Plot Summary
    The Prologue declares that there will be no serious matter
in the play and that "honest mirth" is its only raison-d'etre.
The Vice, Jack Juggler, has resolved to revenge himself on the
boy-servant Jenkin Careaway, who has been wasting his time
playing while on errands for Master Bongrace and Dame Coy.
Careaway's excuse to Dame Coy for tardiness is that he was
watching Master Bongrace flirt with other ladies. He is about
to knock on his master's gate when Jack stops him. Jack,
wearing clothes identical to those of Jenkin and familiar with
his every action that day, bullies the confused boy into believing that he is not himself and that Jack is, in fact, Jenkin
Careaway. Jack leaves the totally perplexed Jenkin to seek

out his mistress Dame Coy. Having been forewarned by
Alison Trip-and-Go of Jenkin's delinquency, Dame Coy
refuses to sympathize with Jenkin's identity crisis and sends
him off to Master Bongrace. Jack boasts to the audience of
the fun he has had with Jenkin and adds that he is reinstated
in his duties. Contrary to the promise of the Prologue that
the play will concern itself only with "honest mirth," the
Epilogue gives in to moralizing on the theme of deluding the
innocent.

Comments

Jack Juggler, a school drama, is a hybrid farce based on the
first part of the *Amphitruo* of Plautus. There is in Jack
Juggler an early example on the English stage of the dis-
appearing motive. As a Vice, Jack does not need motivation
to trick Jenkin, but, as a real person, he should have a reason
for so acting. The author indicates there is a reason for Jack's
dislike of Jenkin, but does not disclose it. An early member
of a great family of stage intriguers, Jack is too much a
morality type to submit to motivation in the modern sense.

Critical Studies

Marienstras, R. *"Jack Juggler:* Aspects de la conscience
    individuelle dans une farce du 16e siècle." *EA,* 16:321-332
    (1963).
Smith, G. C. Moore. *"Jacke Jugeler,* ll. 256-259." *MLR,*
    10:375 (1915).
Voisine, Jacques. "A propos de *Jack Juggler." EA,* 18:166
    (1965). Reply by R. Marienstras, pp. 167-168.
Williams, W. H. "The Date and Authorship of *Jacke Jugeler."
    MLR,* 7:289-295 (1912).

XX. JOHN THE EVANGELIST, 1520-57
(Anonymous)

Here begynneth the enterlude of Iohan the Euangelyst.
John Waley, n.d.

Editions
Farmer, 1907.
*W. W. Greg. *MSR,* 1907.

Dramatis Personae

Saint John the Evangelist	Actio
Eugenio	Evil Counsel
Irisdision	Idleness

Length of the play: 653 lines.

Plot Summary

The action of this short play consists of three sermons preached by Irisdision and St. John the Evangelist to Eugenio, a rich young man, and his friend Actio, also an energetic pleasure-seeker. Eugenio tells Actio of the sermon he has just heard which exhorted him to seek out the road to salvation. They leave and resolve to return by prime to hear John preach. In the meantime, Evil Counsel reveals himself in boastful self-description typical of the Vice he is. We learn that he is looking in England for someone to serve, or, more accurately, someone to serve as a new victim. He engages in bawdy conversation with the dupe Idleness which leads to the usual fight. Reconciled, they leave to find pleasures elsewhere, thus avoiding a sermon to be given by John. Eugenio and Actio listen to John preach on the New Testament parable of the Pharisee and the Publican, and are converted from their love of pleasure and money to the love of God and his kingdom.

56

Comments
  John the Evangelist is an early hybrid play.

Critical Studies
Bradley, Henry. "Textual Notes on *The Enterlude of John the Evangelist.*" *MLR,* 2:350-352 (1907).
Williams, W. H. "Irisdision, in the *Interlude of Johan the Evangelist.*" *MLR,* 3:369-371 (1908).

XXI. KING DARIUS, 1559-65
(Anonymous)

A Pretie new Enterlude both pithie & pleasaunt of the Story of Kyng Daryus, Beinge taken out of the third and fourth Chapter of the thyrd booke of Esdras. Imprynted at London, in Fleet Street, beneath the Conduite, at the sygne of St. John Evangelyst, by Thomas Colwell. Anno Domini MDLXV.

Editions
Brandl.
J. S. Farmer. *The Tudor Facsimile Texts.* London and Edinburgh, 1909.
*Farmer, 1906.

Dramatis Personae

The Prolocutor

Iniquity	Charity
Importunity	Partiality
Equity	King Darius
Agreeable	Perplexity

Preparatus	Curiosity
Juda	Persia
Media	Ethiopia
Constancy	Optimates
Anagnostes	Stipator Primus
Stipator Secundus	Zorobabell

Six persons may easily play it.

Length of the play: 1,605 lines.

Plot Summary

The Prologue tells of a banquet and then a contest sponsored by King Darius which will be the subject of the play. The entire first scene, nevertheless, consists of the fruitless efforts of Charity and Equity to reform Iniquity, the Vice, and his companions Partiality and Importunity. Charity, Equity, and, later on, Constancy represent English Protestantism, while Iniquity, Partiality, and Importunity favor the old religion because it promotes their own evil deeds.

The action of the second scene turns to King Darius and his court. Agreeable and Preparatus, servants of the King, welcome their master who then bids his two advisers Perplexity and Curiosity to prepare a banquet. Ethiopia, Persia, Juda, and Media, the invited guests of the King, eat a hurried meal and leave the stage to Iniquity and the other allegorical figures in the play. Admitting himself to be the son of the Pope, Iniquity first argues with his comrades, and then, abandoned by his friends, he takes on Charity, Equity, and Constancy, who attempt once more his conversion. He dashes off when someone tries to burn him by hurling fire in his direction. Once thanks are given to God for the destruction of the Vice, the virtues make way for King Darius and his court.

Having overheard three of his bodyguard debating while stationed in his chamber, the King has resolved to hear them individually and to award great prizes to the winner. The debate is on the subject of the strongest thing in the world. Stipator Primus argues for the strength of wine, Stipator Secundus opts for the strength of the King, and Zorobabell declares for the strength of women and love, and then for the strength of God's truth. King Darius declares Zorobabell the winner, and allows him to rebuild Jerusalem. The virtues appear once again to commend Zorobabell for constancy, and to condemn the other contestants as false and flattering servants. They end the play wishing that Queen Elizabeth may remain faithful to religious reform.

Comments

The source of *King Darius,* a hybrid play, is the apocryphal Book of Esdras. The play shares the apprehension of many of the English people over the possibility of a Catholic restoration.

Other Protestant plays:
> *Conflict of Conscience* (No. IX).
> *King John* (No. XXII).
> *New Custom* (No. XL).
> *Three Laws* (No. XLIX).

XXII. KING JOHN, 1530-36
(John Bale)

John King of England. MS first printed by Collier.

Editions
J. P. Collier. Camden Society. London, 1838.
*Manly, I.
J. S. Farmer. *Dramatic Writings of John Bale.* 1907.

W. Bang. *Materialien,* XXV, 1909.

J. H. P. Pafford and W. W. Greg. *MSR,* 1931.

Adams, Barry B. *King John.* San Marino, Calif.: Huntington Library, 1969.

Dramatis Personae

King John	Private Wealth
England	Dissimulation
Clergy	Raymundus
Sedition	Simon of Swynsett
Civil Order	Usurped Power
Steven Langton	The Pope
Communality	Interpreter
Nobility	Treason
Cardinal Pandulphus	Verity

Imperial Majesty

(The Pope, Cardinal, Stephen Langton, Raymundus, and Simon of Swynsett need not be considered separate characters. Thus, Private Wealth becomes the Cardinal; Usurped Power plays the role of Pope; Dissimulation, true to his name, becomes first the monk Raymundus, and then Simon of Swynsett; Sedition plays Stephen Langton. Therefore, as Craik argues [*Tudor Interlude,* p. 32], there are not really nineteen roles to fill but fourteen. Because of Bale's extensive revision of the play after many years, technical questions, such as doubling, present special difficulty.)

Length of the play: 2,656 lines.

Plot Summary

Once King John has introduced himself and stated the extent of his domain, England presents him with a serious problem. She complains that she is a widow sorely misused by the hypocritical and mundane clergy. At the entrance of Sedition, the Vice, the conversation turns to the Pope — "the bore of Rome." Sedition, the special friend of the Pope, takes the pontiff's side, but succeeds only in painting an even blacker portrait of both the Holy Father and of the Catholic Church which has caused the separation of England from her spouse God the Father. To remedy the situation, King John resolves to call the Nobility, the Clergy, and the lawyers to a Parliament, and, this failing, to take matters into his own hands. Sedition pits his forces against the King when, in a conversation about the Church, he declares that the nobility is under the control of the Church and will not oppose her influence. Clergy, Nobility, and Civil Order gather around the King, who accuses them of working against England's interests. All promise obedience to the King; when he leaves, Clergy confirms his adherence to the old ways.

Sedition prepares for the conflict with the King by summoning other vices to his aid. The first is his cousin Dissimulation, who shares with Sedition common ancestors named Falsehood, Privy Treason, Infidelity, and the Antichrist Pope. To help restore the abbeys whose existence has been recently jeapardized, Dissimulation offers his child Private Wealth, a monk who has been promoted from the lowly position of cellarer through the hierarchy and is now about to be made cardinal. Along with Private Wealth comes Usurped Power. Carrying Sedition in on their backs to indicate his domination over them, the vices then plot to subdue King John by means of interdict and excommunication. As a first step Usurped Power, Private Wealth, and Sedition dress as the Pope, Cardinal Pandulfus, and a monk and curse the King. The Interpreter reviews the action thus far and summarizes that to come. (These lines of the Interpreter are an insertion in Bale's own hand.)

While Clergy, Nobility, Sedition, and Civil Order promote rebellion, King John, alone on stage, nurses his grudge against the Church. He is then confronted by Cardinal Pandulphus (Private Wealth), who remonstrates with the King over the installation of Steven Langton at Canterbury. When all

XXII

England is put under interdict, the King tries to reason with
Clergy, Nobility, and Civil Order, but fails to change their
position. Greatly dejected, England and blind Communality
lament their supression by the powerful Church. Communality is forced to obey Pandulphus, but England vows fidelity
to the King. When the whole realm is threatened with invas-
ion, King John reluctantly gives up his crown and promises to
pay heavy taxes both to Rome and to the English Church.
Posing as the monk Simon of Swynsett and absolved in advance by Sedition, Dissimulation poisons the King in the
presence of England. Verity eulogizes the dead King and
causes Clergy, Nobility, and Civil Order to repent. Imperial
Majesty reprimands the three estates and exiles Dissimulation,
Private Wealth, and Usurped Power. Unaware of the conversion of his allies, Sedition indulges in a proud explanation of
his evil methods and those of the Pope. He is quickly hanged.
The play ends with thanks to God for the enlightened times
of Queen Elizabeth.

Comments

King John is a very anti-Catholic hybrid play. The homage
to Queen Elizabeth at the end is the result of the revision in
Bale's hand made probably in 1561.

Other "estates" plays:
> *Cobbler's Prophesy* (No. VII).
> *Looking Glass for London and England* (No. XXVII).
> *Play of the Weather* (No. LVI).
> *Satire of the Three Estates* (No. XLV).
> *Three Ladies of London* (No. XLVIII).
> *Three Lords and Three Ladies of London* (No. L).
> *Tide Tarrieth No Man* (No. LI).

Other Protestant plays:
> *Conflict of Conscience* (No. IX).
> *King Darius* (No. XXI).
> *New Custom* (No. XL).
> *Three Laws* (No. XLIX).

Critical Studies

Adams, Barry B. "Doubling in Bale's *King Johan.*" *SP,* 62:111-120 (1965).

———— "John Bale's *King Johan,* Edited with an Introduction and Notes." *DA,* 25:4696 (1965).

Barke, Herbert. *Bale's Kynge Johan und sein Verhaltnis zur zeitgenossischen Geschichtschreibung.* Berlin: K. Triltsch, 1937.

Blatt, Thora B. *The Plays of John Bale: A Study of Ideas, Technique and Style.* Copenhagen: G. E. C. Gad, 1968.

le Boutillier, Mrs. Martin. "Bale's *Kynge Johan* and *The Troublesome Raigne.*" *MLN,* 36:55-57 (1921).

Cason, Clarence. "Additional Lines for Bale's *King Johan.*" *JEGP,* 27:42-50 (1928).

Davies, W. T. "A Bibliography of Bale." In *Oxford Bibliographical Society, Proceedings and Papers,* 5:203-279 (1936-39).

Duncan, Robert Lee. "Protestant Themes and Theses in the Drama of John Bale." *DA,* 25:2957 (1964).

Elson, John. "Studies in the King John Plays." In *Joseph Quincy Adams, Memorial Studies.* Ed. James McManaway et al. Washington: The Folger Library, 1948, pp. 183-197.

Greg. W. W. "Bale's *Kynge Johan.*" *MLN,* 36:505 (1921).

Miller, Edwin. "The Roman Rite in Bale's *King John.*" *PMLA,* 64:802-822 (1949).

Pafford, J. H. P. "Bale's *King John.*" *JEGP,* 30:176-178 (1931).

Wallerstein, Ruth. "King John in Fact and Fiction." University of Pennsylvania Dissertation, 1917.

XXIII. LIBERALITY AND PRODIGALITY, 1567-68
(Anonymous)

A Pleasant Comedie, Shewing the contention betweene Liberalitie and Prodigalitie. As it was playd before her Maiestie. Simon Stafford for George Vincent, 1602.

Editions
Dodsley, VIII.
*W. W. Greg. *MSR,* 1913.

Dramatis Personae

The Prologue	Equity
Vanity, Fortune's chief	Liberality, chief Steward to
servant	Virtue
Prodigality, suitor for	Captain [Weldon]
Money	Courtier
Postilion, his servant	Lame Soldier
Host	Constables with hue and cry
Tenacity	Tipstaves
Dandaline	Sheriff
Tom Tosse	Clerk
Dick Dicer	Crier
Fortune	Judge
Money, her son	Epilogue
Virtue	

(Needed also are musicians attending Fortune and Kings to draw her chariot.)

Length of the Play: 1,352 lines.

Plot Summary
Bedecked in bright feathers, Vanity announces the coming of her "sovereign dame" Fortune, and tells of the emulation existing between Fortune and Dame Virtue. The action of the play gets under way as Prodigality and Postilion stop at an inn

late at night and are joined by Vanity and Tenacity. The latter is searching for Fortune who, he hopes, will be pleased to grant him riches. The scene turns to Virtue and Equity, who lament the popularity of Fortune, but, like all virtues, they are resigned and patient. At their departure, Fortune herself enters with much pomp and expresses the desire for a final and decisive confrontation with Virtue. The two contrary figures of Prodigality and Tenacity both plead in word and song to Lady Fortune for the possession of Money. True to her fickle nature, Fortune for no particular reason gives Money to Prodigality, but promises Tenacity that his day may come. Tom Tosse and Dick Dicer, two gamblers in search of a generous friend, eagerly join Prodigality and Money at the inn where they all are waited on by the hostess Dandaline. The scene changes momentarily to the forces of good. Virtue's servant Liberality delivers a sermon against Fortune and encourages Captain Weldon and the Courtier to rely on Virtue and not on Fortune in their respective careers. Thoroughly disappointed with the incessant handling he has received while with Prodigality, Money, now threadbare and emaciated from too much activity, willingly transfers to Tenacity, who promises to keep him out of use and locked up in a coffer. Under the instigation of Dick Dicer, Prodigality, angry at the loss of his Money, lays siege to Fortune's castle, but he falls off his ladder when Fortune throws a halter around his neck. Still undaunted, Prodigality steals Money back from Tenacity and is arrested by the sheriff. Money, fat from lack of use, gladly is turned over to Liberality from whom he can expect intelligent treatment. Liberality makes good use of Money in rewarding Captain Weldon and the Lame Soldier for their services to the realm. Prodigality is found guilty of theft and the murder of Tenacity, but the death sentence is not carried out when he gives signs of reformation.

Comments

Liberality and Prodigality is a social morality much concerned with Queen Elizabeth's financial policies. The appearance of the character Fortune is limited in the interludes to *Liberality and Prodigality* and *The Longer Thou Livest, the More Fool Thou Art* (No. XXVI).

Other "social" plays:
  Albion Knight (No. I).
  All for Money (No. II).
  Impatient Poverty (No. XVIII).
  Like Will to Like (No. XXV).
  Wealth and Health (No. LV).

See *Cobbler's Prophesy* (No. VII), for a list of the "estates" plays, all of which are "social" pieces.

XXIV. LIFE AND REPENTANCE OF MARY MAGDALENE
c. 1550
(Lewis Wager)

A new Enterlude, neuer before this tyme imprinted, entreating of the Life and Repentaunce of Marie Magdalene: not only godlie, learned and fruitefull, but also well furnished with pleasaunt myrth and pastime, very delectable for those which shall heare or reade the same. Made by the learned clarke Lewis Wager. John Charlwood, 1566.

Edition
F. I. Carpenter. *The Life and Repentance of Mary Magdalene.* Chicago, 1904.

Dramatis Personae

Infidelity the Vice	The Law
Mary Magdalene	Knowledge of Sin
Pride of Life	Christ Jesus
Cupidity	Faith
Carnal Concupiscence	Repentance
Simon the Pharisee	Justification
Malicious Judgment	Love

(The title page says that four may perform the play. Carpenter points out that in reality five are necessary for performance. See his Introduction, p. xvii.)

Length of the play: 2,052 lines.

Plot Summary

The Prologue emphasizes the homiletic purpose of this play which is, of course, based on the gospel story of Mary Magdalene. Infidelity, the Vice, proudly announces his alias of "Moysaicall Justice" which he uses among the Jews, but assures the audience that he is in reality the "head of all iniquitie." Pride, Cupidity, and Carnal Concupiscence boast of their evil natures and inform Infidelity that they are already in the heart of the young heiress Mary Magdalene, in spite of her virtuous upbringing. To facilitate their influence on Mary, Pride takes the name of Nobility and Honor, and Concupiscence, Cupidity, and Infidelity become Pleasure, Utility, and Prudence.

True to his promise, Infidelity introduces the vices as suitable companions to Mary, who eagerly accepts their doctrine of proud and sensual behavior. When the three vices take their leave, Mary accompanies Infidelity to Jerusalem. While she leads a life of sin, Simon the Pharisee, Malicious Judgment, and then Infidelity dressed as a Pharisee plot the destruction of Christ and Mary. Law of God, carrying the Tables of the Law, rebukes Mary, whose conscience begins to bother her. Infidelity denounces Law of God in an effort to

67

retain the loyalty of the sinful woman. Before being driven off by Infidelity, Knowledge of Sin also pricks Mary's conscience, but she tends toward despair. Christ offers Mary the consolation of his mercy and expels Infidelity, who departs amidst a great wailing of the devils. Mary, repentant and converted, is lead off by Faith and Repentance.

Christ is invited to Simon's house for dinner, where he disputes with Malicious Judgment and Infidelity, and declares himself the Son of God. Mary washes the feet of Christ, who then publicly forgives her sins and delivers the parable of the two debtors. The banquet breaks up, but Infidelity and Malicious Judgment seek to collect condemning evidence against Christ. The Protestant nature of the play becomes more apparent in its ending. Mary receives instruction from Justification, who interprets the words of Christ "Many sins are forgiven her for she loved much." Justification maintains that in reality it was faith alone that justified Mary and not love. Love, the result of faith, enters, and, together with Justification, reviews Mary's life and repentance.

Comments

The Life and Repentance of Mary Magdalene is a "virtue" play. The plot, taken from the gospel (Luke vii-viii), relates to a theme often found in many continental plays — that of the delinquent child. See, for example, *The Disobedient Child* (Dodsley II) and *Nice Wanton* (No. XLI). The influence on *The Life and Repentance of Mary Magdalene* of Bale's *Three Laws* (No. XLIX) should be noted; the Vice Infidelity appears in both plays, as does the carrying by Law of the Tables of the Law.

Other "virtue" plays:

Appius and Virginia (No. III).
Godly Queen Hester (No. XIV).
Patient and Meek Grissill (No. XLII).
Virtuous and Godly Susanna (No. LIV).

Critical Studies

Blackburn, Ruth Harriett. "Tudor Biblical Drama." *DA*,
17:1746-1747 (1957).

Hoffmann, M. N. *Die Magdalenenszenen im geistlichen Spiel
des deutschen Mittelalters.* Wursburg: Konrad Triltsch,
1933.

Knoll, Friedrich Otto. *Die Rolle der Maria Magdalene im
geistlichen Spiel des Mittelalters.* Berlin and Leipsig:
W. de Gruyter, 1934.

Lewis, Leon Eugene. "The Play of Mary Magdalene." *DA*,
23:4685-4686 (1963).

McDermott, John James. "Mary Magdalene in English Literature from 1500-1650." *DA*, 25:5260-5261 (1965).

Schmidt, Karl. "Die Digby-Spiele." *Anglia*, 8:371-404 (1885).

XXV. LIKE WILL TO LIKE, 1562-68
(Ulpian Fulwell)

*An Enterlude Intituled Like wil to like quod the Deuel to the
Colier very godly and ful of pleasant mirth. Wherein is declared
not onely what punishment followeth those that wil rather
followe licentious liuing, then to esteeme & followe good
councel: and what great benefits and commodities they
receive that apply them vnto vertuous liuing and good
exercises.* Made by Vlpian Fulwel. John Allde, 1568.

Editions
Dodsley, III.
*Farmer, 1906.

Dramatis Personae

Five may easily play this Interlude

For one
{ The Prologue
Tom Tosspot
Hankin Hangman
Tom Collier

For one
{ Lucifer
Ralph Roister
Good Fame
Severity

For one
{ Hance
Virtuous Life
God's Promise
Cuthbert Cutpurse

For one
{ Philip Fleming
Pierce Pickpurse
Honor

Nichol Newfangle, the Vice

Length of the play: 1,277 lines.

Plot Summary

Objecting to the intermingling of good men with evil, Lucifer commands Nichol Newfangle, the Vice, always to join men with their own kind. Nichol obliges his master by finding him a suitable companion in the dishonest dealer in coal Tom Collier. Next, Tom Tosspot is paired with Ralph Roister. Each tries to prove himself more a knave than the other, but the judge, Nichol Newfangle, declares them to be equal in knavery. Two drunkards Hance and Philip Fleming are brought together in still another exemplification of the titular proverb "similis similem sibi quaerit." At their departure Nichol sings a song prophesying the downfall of the evil companions at his own hands.

Nichol's next plot concerns two pickpockets Cuthbert Cutpurse and Pierce Pickpurse to whom he promises a vacant piece of property called the "two legged mare." They are joined by Virtuous Living in a brief encounter which points out the corollary of the play's proverbial title — that the virtuous and the ungodly do not mix for long. Virtuous Life joins his own group of godly companions, Good Fame, God's Promise, and Honor.

The passage of time witnesses the degradation of Tom Tosspot and Ralph Roister. Both are reduced to beggary, the result of gambling and drinking. Having offered themselves to all as examples of the consequences in this world of licentious living, they leave but only after giving Nichol a beating for having lead them astray. Nichol next helps Judge Severity capture two fugitives from Justice who turn out to be none other than Cuthbert Cutpurse and Pierce Pickpurse. By throwing halters around their necks, Nichol makes them into "two legged mares" about to come into the property promised earlier — the region of Death. They too offer themselves to parents and children as examples of the results of evil living. Although Pierce calls on God for mercy, we learn from Nichol that he and his friend meet death cursing. Philip Fleming and Hance are stricken with the gout. Lucifer enters to carry Nichol to hell on his back. Virtuous Life, Good Fame, and Honor close the play with prayers for the Queen, Lords, and Commons and with a song.

Comments

Like Will to Like is a social morality pointing out the results in this world of greed and evil companions. The bifurcation of the Mankind figure can be seen here in Virtuous Life on the one hand, and the evil companions on the other. The Figures of Honor and Reward show this morality to be secular, as do the results of sin — beggary, sickness, punishment at the hands of the law.

Other "social" plays:
    Albion Knight (No. I).
    Impatient Poverty (No. XVIII).

Liberality and Prodigality (No. XXIII).
Wealth and Health (No. LV).
Other plays with a bifurcated Mankind figure:
    Enough is as Good as a Feast (No. XI).
    Glass of Government (No. XIII).
    Nice Wanton (No. XLI).
    Tide Tarrieth No Man (No. LI).
    Trial of Treasure (No. LIII).
See *Cobbler's Prophesy* (No. VII) for a list of the "estates" plays, all of which are "social" pieces.
    Coming of Death (Appendix I).

Critical Studies
Sabol, Andrew J. "A Three-Man Song in Fulwell's *Like Will to Like* at the Folger." *RN,* 10:139-142 (1957).

XXVI. THE LONGER THOU LIVEST, THE MORE FOOL THOU ART, 1560-68
(W. Wager)

A very mery and Pythie Commedie, called The longer thou liuest the more foole thou art. A Myrrour very necessarie for youth, and specially for such as are like to come to dignitie and promotion: As it maye well appeare in the Matter folowynge. Newly compiled by W. Wager. William How for Richard Jones, n.d.

Editions
Brandl. *Jahrbuch,* XXXVI (1900).
*R. Mark Benbow. *Regents Renaissance Drama Series.*
   (University of Nebraska) Lincoln, Neb., 1967.

Dramatis Personae
    Four may play it easily
Prologue   ⎫
Exercitation   ⎪
Wrath   ⎬   for one
Cruelty   ⎪
God's Judgment ⎭
Moros   ⎫
Fortune   ⎬ for another
Discipline   ⎫
Incontinence ⎪
Impiety   ⎬ for another
Confusion   ⎭
Piety   ⎫
Idleness   ⎪
Ignorance ⎬ for another
People   ⎭

Length of the play: 1,977 lines.

Plot Summary
    Having suffered from an exceptionally poor upbringing, the young fool Moros shows himself to be completely scatterbrained. Realizing that the chances for Moros' reformation are slight, Discipline, Piety, and Exercitation nonetheless attempt his initiation into the pious life. Moros leaves with his new mentor Piety, while Discipline and Exercitation exchange pessimistic comments as to his outcome. The vices Idleness, Incontinence, and Wrath plot the downfall of the young fool, but they too, like the virtues, soon realize that Moros needs no prodding down the broad road to damnation. They adopt new names — Pastime (Idleness), Pleasure (Incontinence), Manhood (Wrath) — but Wrath points out that even this usual procedure is in this case unnecessary:
      In good faith littel needeth this device;
      To be called by our names is as good

. . . . . .
He discerneth not clean from unclean;
His mind is all set on foolery.

Moros willingly accepts the life of pleasure described to him
by the vices, but is unable to face up to Discipline. Wrath explains that fear is always the lot of young men inexperienced
with women. They bring Moros, therefore, to Pleasure for his
initiation in sex. Incontinence reports the treatment given
Moros by the prostitutes, and then elicits the help of proud
Fortune to ruin him further.

Sporting a "foolish beard" as a sign of Fortune's favor and
also of his adulthood, Moros is victimized by three more disguised vices — Philosophy (Impiety), Prudence (Cruelty), and
Antiquity (Ignorance). Moros, now a thoroughly ridiculous
gallant, confronts Discipline with great bravado, but bungles
at pulling his sword out of its sheath. At the suggestion of
Ignorance, he decides that descretion is the better part of
valor and leaves.

Representing those with whom Moros has come in contact,
People denounces him, as do God's Judgment and Confusion.
Once again the blame for Moros' ill-spent life is laid on his
family. When his worldly garments are removed, the vesture
of a fool appears underneath. Confusion carries the still ignorant but now old fool Moros on his back to hell.

The remaining portion of the play is given over to a review
in learned terms of the opposite paths to perdition and to
salvation. Once a soul has piety, he can be instructed in wisdom, which will strengthen his will and confirm him in
godliness.

Comments

The Longer Thou Livest is a Protestant morality. Moros
represents not humanity, but only those of whom it must be
said "that nothing can their crokedness rectify" (Prologue),
men on the wrong side of the Calvinist coin of predestination.
The appearance of the character Fortune is limited in the

interludes to *The Longer Thou Livest* and *Liberality and Prodigality* (No. XXIII).
   See *Enough is as Good as a Feast* (No. XI).
      Coming of Death (Appendix I).

XXVII. A LOOKING GLASS FOR LONDON AND ENGLAND, c. 1590
(Thomas Lodge and Robert Greene)

A Looking Glasse for London and England. Made by Thomas Lodge Gentleman, and Robert Greene. Thomas Creede, 1594.

Editions

Alexander Dyce. *The Dramatic Works of Robert Greene.* London, 1831.
          The Dramatic and Political Works of Robert Greene and George Peele. London, 1861.
Edmund W. Gosse. *The Complete Works of Thomas Lodge.* Hunterian Club Edition. Glasgow, 1878-82. Reprinted, New York: Russell and Russell, 1963.
Alexander B. Grossart. *Life and Complete Works of Robert Greene.* London, 1881-86.
J. Churton Collins. *The Plays and Poems of Robert Greene.* Oxford, 1905.
Thomas H. Dickenson. *The Complete Plays of Robert Greene.* London, 1909.
John S. Farmer. *A Looking Glass for London and England.* Tudor Facsimile Texts. Amersham, 1914.
*W. W. Greg. *A Looking Glass for London and England.* MSR, 1932.

Dramatis Personae
 Rasni, King of Nineveh, or of Assyria
 The King of Cilicia
 The King of Crete
 The King of Paphlagonia
 Radagon, a courtier, son of Alcon
 Remelia, sister to Rasni
 Alvida, wife of Paphlagonia
 An Angel
 Oseas, the prophet, as Chorus
 A Smith
 Adam, a clown, his man
 Two Ruffians
 A Usurer
 Thrasibulus, a young gentleman
 Alcon, a poor man
 Magi
 Lawyer
 A Judge
 A Lord
 Jonas, the prophet
 A Master Mariner
 A Sailor
 A Merchant of Tharsus
 Samia, wife of Alcon
 Clesiphon, their son
 The Smith's wife
 The Governor of Joppa
 The Priest of the Sun
 A man disguised as a Devil
 An Evil Angel
 Ladies
 Two Searchers
   Lords, Ladies, Ruffians, Sailors, Merchants

Length of the play: 2,409 lines.

Plot Summary

Exulting from his recent victory over Jeroboam of Jerusalem, King Rasni of Nineveh enters in triumph and receives the praise of the Kings of Cilicia, Crete, and Paphlagonia. Rasni's sister Remelia offers him congratulations and accepts his proposal of marriage. Objections are posed by the King of Crete to such an incestuous union, but he is rebuked by the flattering courtier Radagon. We learn from Radagon that Rasni is above all law and morality. Rasni commands all the court to celebrate and gives specific orders to indulge in all forms of excessive conduct with no fear of royal displeasure.

An Angel sets the prophet Oseas on a throne overlooking Nineveh. Oseas has been removed miraculously from Jerusalem after having unsuccessfully preached there. He is commanded to note all the outrageous sins of the Ninevites which he will in time use as evidence of the world's wickedness. Oseas first witnesses Adam, the Smith's servant, and his friends who are all bent on finding ale and women. Next, he sees a Usurer forclose on Thrasibulus, a gentleman, and Alcon, a poor man. After each scene Oseas speaks in choral comment addressing the people of London in an appeal to see their own sins mirrored in those of the Ninevites.

Richly dressed for the wedding, Remelia converses with Alvida, her lady-in-waiting. She exhibits the same inordinate pride and arrogance as her brother and fiance Rasni. The wedding never takes place. Having entered the royal tent, Remelia is struck down by lightning. At first Rasni is somewhat sobered by this obvious sign of divine displeasure. Radagon points out that Alvida is as beautiful as was Remelia, and that, with her husband Paphlagonia absent, she is readily available.

Thrasibulus and Alcon have now found a Lawyer and prepare to bring suit against the Usurer before the Judge. The Usurer, however, bribes both the Judge and the opposing Lawyer and is awarded the patrimony of Thrasibulus and Alcon's cow. While the Usurer and Lawyer are entertained at dinner at the Judge's house, Thrasibulus and Alcon seek further help from Alcon's son at court.

In a drunken fight, Adam kills one of his cronies. Rasni and his court happen by and find the dead body. Unable to elicit any information from Adam, they allow the Smith to take him home. The King of Paphlagonia arrives to reproach Rasni for taking his wife as a paramour. Feigning contrition, Alvida tricks Paphlagonia into drinking a goblet of wine as a pledge of his forgiveness of her. The wine, of course, is poisoned and Paphlagonia dies cursing adulterous women. Once again, Oseas reminds the people of London that they too are guilty of murder and adultery and that the sword of justice is about to fall.

An Angel commands Jonas in God's name to preach in Nineveh. Jones judges, however, that his efforts would only lead to more wickedness and decides to flee to Joppa. Meanwhile, Alcon and his starving family and Thrasibulus seek out Alcon's son at court who is none other than evil Radagon. Radagon rejects them outright and influences Rasni to banish them all. Samia, Radagon's mother, formally curses him and triumphs when flames spring up consuming her depraved son. Marveling at Radagon's death, Rasni wonders if there might be someone with powers greater than his own. He is comforted by a Soothsayer who directs his attention back to the beautiful Alvida.

The Smith discovers that Adam has been having an affair with his wife. He tries to beat him but is himself in the end drubbed by Adam. The Merchants, Master Mariner, and crew of the ship that Jonas boarded enter shipwreaked. They announce their conversion to Judaism because Jonas' God saved them from a terrible storm. Jonas, in the meantime, having been thrown overboard, is cast up from the whale's belly and is now obedient to God's command to convert the Ninevites.

Alvida has become enamored with the King of Cilicia whom she declares to be her true love. Rasni joins them but

is interrupted by the Priest of the Sun who tells of walking
ghosts and bloodstained statues. The Sages, however, interpret these signs to signify danger only to Rasni's foes. Comforted, Rasni prepares a feast for Alvida and the nobles.

While conducting his mistress home late at night Adam
confronts a man disguised as a devil. Adam is not at all
frightened and even threatens to beat the devil off with a
club. Next, Thrasibulus and Alcon tell of the life of beggary
they are forced to lead. They take possession of the discarded
clothes of the would-be devil and sell them to the Usurer.
Jonas now enters preaching destruction unless they repent.
Thrasibulus and Alcon and his family admit their sins and
even the Usurer is confounded by guilt. Oseas for the last
time implores the people of London to learn from the
Ninevites. The Angel then tells him that he will not see the
destruction of Nineveh, but will be immediately carried back
to Jerusalem.

Jonas disrupts Rasni's banquet with his prophesy. Rasni
immediately sends away his false Sages, confesses his sins,
and dresses himself in sackcloth. Alvida, likewise, takes her
ladies aside for prayers of reparation. A victim of despair the
Usurer displays a halter and dagger — the instruments of suicide. He resists the temptation of the Evil Angel to take his
own life and prays for forgiveness. Only Adam refuses to
obey the King's edict to fast and pray. He tries to outwit the
two Searchers who find him, but is taken with his pockets
full of food. Rather than fast five days, Adam agrees to be
hanged. Jonas informs the King that they have fasted suffi-
ciently. The Usurer refunds all those whom he has wronged.
Rasni establishes Judaism in Nineveh and marries Alvida.
Jonas addresses the last lines of the play to the people of
London calling on them to see themselves and their own sins
in its action.

Comments

A late play, *A Looking Glass for London and England* is a

hybrid "estates" morality. The biblical allegory is taken from the Book of Jonah.

Other "estates" plays:
> *Cobbler's Prophesy* (No. VII).
> *King John* (No. XXII).
> *Play of the Weather* (No. LVI).
> *Satire of the Three Estates* (No. XLV).
> *Three Ladies of London* (No. XLVIII).
> *Three Lords and Three Ladies of London* (No. L).
> *Tide Tarrieth No Man* (No. LI).

Critical Studies

Baskervill, C. R. "A Prompt Copy of *A Looking Glass for London and England." MP,* 30:29-51 (1932).

Clugston, George Alan. *"A Looking Glass for London and England,* By Thomas Lodge and Robert Greene. A Critical Edition." University of Michigan Dissertation, 1967.

Hayashi, Tetsumaro. "An Edition of *A Looking Glass for London and England* by Thomas Lodge and Robert Greene." *DA,* 29:4457A (1968).

_____ *A Textual Study of A Looking Glass for London and England by Thomas Lodge and Robert Greene.* Ball State University Monograph 17. Muncie, Ind., 1969.

Law, Robert. *"A Looking Glass* and the Scriptures." *University of Texas Studies* (1931), pp. 31-47.

_____ "Two Parallels to Green and Lodge's *Looking Glass." MLN,* 26:146-148 (1911).

McNeir, Waldo F. "The Date of *A Looking Glass for London." N&Q,* 200:282-283 (1955).

Parr, Johnstone and I.A. Shapiro. *Instructions to Editors of the Works of Robert Greene.* Birmingham, England: The Shakespeare Institute, 1959.

Parr, Johnstone et al. *List of Editions, Copies, and Locations of the Works of Robert Greene.* Birmingham, England: The Shakespeare Institute, 1958.

Rae, Wesley. *Thomas Lodge.* New York: Twayne, 1967.

Ryan, P. M. *Thomas Lodge, Gentleman.* Hamden, Conn.: The Shoe String Press, 1958.

Swaen, A. E. H. *"A Looking Glass for London and England: Nutmegs and Ginger." MLR*, 33:404-405 (1938).

Tenney, Edward. *Thomas Lodge.* Ithaca: Cornell University Press, 1935. (Reprinted, New York: Russell and Russell, 1969).

XXVIII. LOVE, Play of, 1530-33
(John Heywood)

A play of loue, A newe and a mery enterlude concerning pleasure and payne in loue, made by John Heywood. William Rastell, 1534.

Editions
Brandl.
*J. S. Farmer. *The Dramatic Writings of John Heywood.* 1905.
K. W. Cameron. Raleigh, N. C., 1944.

Dramatis Personae
    The Lover Loved
    The Lover not Loved
    Neither Lover nor Loved, the Vice
    The Woman Beloved not Loving

Length of the play: Approximately 1,400 lines.

Plot Summary
    Having come to an impasse in their debate on the subject

81

of who suffers more pain, Lover not Loved and Woman Beloved not Loving seek a judge to settle the matter. In a similar debate as to who experiences more pleasure, Lover Loved and Neither Lover nor Loved, the Vice, also reach a stalemate. While Lover Loved searches for a judge, Neither Lover nor Loved explains in a long monologue that his present hatred for love and women had its source in a previous unfaithful lover. Lover Loved enters with Lover not Loved and Beloved not Loving, who agree to judge the contest between Lover Loved and Neither Lover nor Loved if these latter two will perform the same service for them. Each debater states his case amidst constant interruptions from the Vice, Neither Lover nor Loved. His own arguments against Lover Loved are bolstered by a prank he plays to prove his point. Leaving to fetch a book, he runs back on stage "carrying a copper tank full of burning squibs and crying 'fire, fire'." He announces that a fire has leveled the very house wherein dwells the beloved of Lover Loved. Grief-stricken, Lover Loved seeks death with his beloved; and the Vice claims to have proven his case. The hoax is revealed, however, and Lover Loved attempts to refute the Vice. They unanimously decide that reason commands them to be satisfied with their own lots in life and to seek first the love of God.

Comments

The Vice, Neither Lover nor Loved, is a significant borrowing from the moralities in this "debate" play.

See *All for Money* (No. II).

Play of the Weather (No. LVI).

Critical Studies

Canzler, David George. "A Concordance to the Dramatic Works of John Heywood." *DA,* 21:3768-3769 (1961).

Craik, T. W. "Experiment and Variety in John Heywood's Plays." *RenD,* 7:6-11 (1964).

Greg, W. W. "An Unknown Edition of *Play of Love.*" *Archiv,*
106:141-143 (1901).

Hillebrand, H. N. "On the Authorship of the Interludes
Attributed to John Heywood." *MP,* 13:267-280 (1915).

La Rosa, Frank E. "A Critical Edition of John Heywood's *A
Play of Love.*" *DA,* 29:2218A (1969).

Phy, Wesley. "The Chronology of John Heywood's Plays."
ES, 14:27-41 (1940).

Reed, A. W. *"The Play of Love,* A Correction." *The Library,*
4th ser., 4:159 (1923).

Schoeck, R. J. "A Common Tudor Expletive and Legal
Parody in Heywood's *Play of Love.*" *N&Q,* 3:375-376
(1956).

_____ "Satire of Wolsey in Heywood's *Play of Love.*"
N&Q, 196:112-114 (1931).

XXIX. LOVE FEIGNED AND UNFEIGNED, 1540-60
(Anonymous)

MS fragment, now in the British Museum.

Edition
A. Esdaile. *Malone Society Collections,* I, i, (1907).

Dramatis Personae
Familiarity
Love Unfeigned
Fellowship
Falsehood
Love Feigned

Length of the fragment: 243 lines.

Plot Summary

Familiarity welcomes Love Unfeigned, who represents proper love, "free from crewell vice," and who is now introduced to Fellowship. Fellowship rejoices that he has two such virtuous companions. Typical of his role as chief instigator of evil, the Vice, Falsehood, delivers a boastful monologue on the subject of his own prominence in the world. He joins with Love Feigned to subvert Fellowship, who happens by. Fellowship finds their arguments in favor of dissimulation and selfishness reasonable, and willingly forsakes a life of virtue for one of merriment. The fragment ends after Falsehood, Feigned Love, and Fellowship have sung a song in celebration of Fellowship's new direction in life.

Comments

Love Feigned and Unfeigned appears to be a Protestant morality.

Critical Studies

Daw, Beatrice. *"Love Feyned and Unfeyned* and the English Anabaptists." *PMLA*, 32:267-291 (1917).

Scragg, Leah Lindsay. *"Love Feigned and Unfeigned:* A Note on the use of Allegory on the Tudor Stage." *ELN*, 3:248-252 (1966).

XXX. LUSTY JUVENTUS, 1547-53
(R. Wever)

An Enterlude called lusty Iuuentus. Lyuely describing the frailtie of youth: of natur prone to vyce: by grace and good counsayll, traynable to vertue. W. Copland, n.d.

Editions
T. Hawkins. *Origin of the English Drama,* I. London, 1733.
*Dodsley, II.
Farmer, 1905.

Dramatis Personae
Four may play it easily, taking such parts as they think best: so that any one take of those parts that be not in place at once.

Messenger	Hypocrisie
Lusty Juventus	Fellowship
Good Counsel	Abominable Living
Knowledge	God's Merciful Promises
Satan the Devil	

Length of the play: 1,167 lines.

Plot Summary
Already past innocence, carefree and fun-seeking Juventus asks Good Counsel the way to the nearest party. Instead of giving him directions, Good Counsel admonishes the youth and converts him from the evils of sinful pleasure. Knowledge instructs Juventus in theology (Protestant), and in the habits of a true Christian — the fear of God, the love of neighbor, the observance of the golden rule, perseverance, reliance on Scripture. Representing the champion of the old ways (Catholicism), the Devil laments the inquisitive tendencies of the young, who recognize the sham of the Church of Rome and follow Protestantism. He enlists the help of Hypocrisy to ensnare the reformed Juventus. While on his way to a sermon, Juventus falls into the clever hands of Hypocrisy, who, under the name of Knowledge, draws the youth away from his godly pastime. At first he resists firmly, but in the end admits that as long as he is not missed by his pious friends he does not object to sporting with Hypocrisy. They are joined by Fellowship and the harlot Abominable Living, who gives

85

Juventus particular attention. Good Counsel for the second time calls back the fallen youth, who, like all contrite Mankind figures, quickly despairs of God's forgiveness. Reassured by God's Promises, Juventus himself delivers a forceful denunciation of sinful living.

Comments

Lusty Juventus, a "youth" play, is a Protestant morality of the reign of Edward VI.

Other "youth" plays:

>*Glass of Government* (No. XIII).
>*Hickscorner* (No. XVI).
>*Marriage of Wit and Wisdom* (No. XXXIV).
>*Misogonus* (No. XXXVI).
>*Nice Wanton* (No. XLI).
>*Wit and Science* (No. LVIII).
>*Youth* (No. LIX).

XXXI. MAGNIFICENCE, 1513-16
(John Skelton)

Magnyfycence, A goodly interlude and a mery deuysed and made by mayster Seklton, poet laureate late deceasyd. Printed in folio c. 1533.

Editions

J. Littledale. Roxburghe Club. London, 1821.
A. Dyce. *Poetical Works of John Skelton,* I. London, 1843.
*R. L. Ramsay. *EETS,* Extra Series, xcviii, London, 1906 (reprinted in 1958).
P. Henderson. *Complete Poems of John Skelton.* London, 1931.

Dramatis Personae
(The grouping of the names of the characters below follows the MS grouping. The characters are also named in the order of their coming on stage.)

Felicity	Cloaked Colusion
Liberty	Courtly Abusion
Measure	Folly
	Adversity
Magnificence	Poverty
Fancy	Despair
Counterfeit Countenance	Mischief
Crafty Conveyance	

Good Hope
Redress
Circumspection
Perseverance

(The aliases used by the vices are as follows: Fancy-Largess, Crafty Conveyance-Sure Surveyance, Cloaked Collusion-Sober Sadness, Counterfeit Countenance-Good Demeanance, Courtly Abusion-Lusty Pleasure, Folly-Conceit.)

Length of the play: 2,567 lines.

Plot Summary
Felicity begins with a monologue stating the moral of the play: that a truly wise ruler will manage his wealth intelligently. But, Felicity continues, the fact is that often rulers leave off Circumspection in favor of Liberty. In a debate with Liberty, Felicity says that Liberty must use restraint (Continence), but Liberty argues that happiness (Felicity) depends on complete freedom. In his role as arbiter, Measure takes the position that moderation is most important to a ruler. When they finally agree that all are necessary to any prince, Magnificence enters and is introduced by Measure to Felicity and Liberty. Once Liberty has been handed over to Measure,

Magnificence begins to converse with Felicity, but Fancy breaks in, and, by means of a forged letter from Circumspection and a false name (Largess), ingratiates himself with the young ruler. Fancy's efforts succeed, and he is brought to the palace having convinced Magnificence that Measure is proper to merchants, but not for princes.

The second section of the play introduces the vices. Counterfeit Countenance speaks a long monologue on current fashions and names those classes of society addicted to them. Fancy, who has recently been made knight under the alias of Largess, returns with Crafty Conveyance. Crafty Conveyance has also secured admittance to Magnificence under the name of Sure Surveyance. They are joined by Cloaked Colusion dressed as a priest and called Sober Sadness. Using the alias of Good Demeanance, Counterfeit Countenance leaves the stage with Fancy and Crafty Conveyance to prepare for their entrance at court. Cloaked Colusion speaks a monologue describing his extensive double-dealing. When Courtly Abusion boasts of his high place at court, Cloaked Colusion plays the courtier to Crafty Conveyance, who has re-entered and they quarrel. Fancy summons Courtly Abusion to court where, as a result of Fancy's efforts, Liberty has been set free and Measure deposed. Courtly Abusion choses Lusty Pleasure as his alias and leaves the stage to Fancy, who delivers a confession of his own scatter-brained character. Folly, Fancy's brother, enters dressed as a fool and the two reminisce about their school days and engage in a bit of mutual deception in which Fancy is cheated. Crafty Conveyance learns to respect Folly when he loses in a verbal argument and a wager. Folly, alias Conceit, Fancy and Crafty Conveyance gather around Magnificence.

Magnificence, now corrupted by his imprudent actions, delivers a self-adulatory monologue proclaiming his disdain for Fortune. Courtly Abusion tempts him to gratify his senses by taking a woman and congratulates wayward Magnificence for renouncing Reason. Measure, under the instigation of

Cloaked Colusion, tries to regain admittance to Magnificence, but is rudely rejected. The court is now in the hands of the false courtiers, and Magnificence has so fallen from his former princely state that he now speaks only nonsense. The scene ends when, at the flight of the false courtiers who have captured Felicity, the truth is made known and grim Adversity enters.

Adversity tells of the humbling of such men as Magnificence whom he then hands over to Poverty. Poverty reminds Magnificence of Lady Fortune, and Liberty only with difficulty recognizes the fallen Prince. Crafty Conveyance, Cloaked Colusion, and Counterfeit Countenance rejoice in their success, but begin to fight among themselves. When they leave for the tavern, Despair "that Adversyte dothe folowe" recommends suicide for Magnificence because his sins are too great for forgiveness. Mischief offers a knife and a halter to Magnificence, but Good Hope rushes in at the last moment to snatch the sword away from the hand of Magnificence and reminds him that no sin is so heinous that it cannot be forgiven. Once Redress has tested the contrition of Magnificence and sent for Circumspection, Magnificence is dressed in a new suit of clothes indicative of his new state. We learn that his sin was caused from believing in others too quickly. The play closes as Magnificence accompanied by his virtuous companions returns to the palace to begin a new life of prosperity.

Comments

Magnificence, the finest contribution of the moralities to literary art, is a prime example of the "speculum principis" tradition. Fancy is the chief Vice. Measure, derived from Aristotle, is the key to moral well-being and earthly happiness.

See *Good Order* (No. XV).
Coming of Death (Appendix I).

Critical Studies

Harris, William O. *Skelton's Magnyfycence and the Cardinal Virtue Tradition.* Chapel Hill: University of North Carolina Press, 1965.

_____ "The Thematic Importance of Skelton's Allusion to Horace in *Magnyfycence." SEL,* 3:9-18 (1963).

_____ "Wolsey and Skelton's *Magnyfycence:* A Re-valuation." *SP,* 57:99-122 (1960).

Hooper, E. S. "Skelton's *Magnificence* and Cardinal Wolsey." *MLN,* 16:426-429 (1901).

Kinsman, Robert S. "Skelton's *Magnyfycence:* The Strategy of the 'Olde Sayde Sawe'." *SP,* 63:99-125 (1966).

Kinsman, Robert S., and Theodore Yonge. *John Skelton: Canon and Census.* Renaissance Society of America, Bibliographies and Indexes 4, Darien Conn.: Monographic Press, 1967.

Rowland, Beryl. "Bone-Ache in Skelton's *Magnyfycence." N&Q,* 11:211 (1964).

West, Michael. "Skelton and the Renaissance Theme of Folly." *PQ,* 50:23-25 (1971).

XXXII. MANKIND, 1461-85
(Anonymous)

Macro MS. now Folger MS. V. a. 354. First published by Brandl, 1898.

Editions
Brandl.
Manly, I.

*F. J. Furnivall and A. W. Pollard. *EETS,* Extra Series, xci,
   London, 1904 (Reprinted in 1924).
J. S. Farmer. *The Tudor Facsimile Texts.* London and Edin-
   burgh, 1907.
Farmer, 1907.
Adams.
Marc Eccles. *EETS,* No. 262, 1969.

Dramatis Personae

Mankind	Nought
Mercy	New-guise
Mischief	Nowadays
Titivillus	

Length of the play: 907 lines.

Plot Summary

   Mercy opens the play with an appeal to the audience to
unite in the salvation of Christ: temptation must be conquered and good works accomplished so that on the last day they
may all be numbered with the "corn" which shall be saved
and not with the "chaff" destined for burning. Mischief, the
Vice, breaks in and puns on Mercy's metaphor of the corn
and chaff, until the flustered Mercy, annoyed at his glib sar-
casm, orders him to leave. Nought, New-guise, and Nowadays,
the three minions of Mischief, enter with their musicians and
begin to sing and dance. Mercy, when invited, refuses to join
in the revelry. After introductions are made all around, Mercy
is again the object of ridicule, this time for his Latinate English. Tired of their company, Mercy regrets the judgment of
God due them in the end and sends the jovial but good-for-
nothing pranksters away.
   Mankind offers an explanation of himself as a composite
of body and soul which are continually at odds. He resolves
to seek Mercy for help and is given the usual advice to resist
temptation and to be moderate. When New-guise, Nought,

and Nowadays interrupt, Mercy takes the opportunity to warn Mankind not only against the three newcomers who have not been to Mass in a year, but also against the devil Titivillus (Totus Villus). Believing he has overcome the flesh, Mankind begins to assume his daily chores as a farmer, but is continually bothered by Nought, New-guise, and Nowadays until he beats them off with a spade. Thanking God for his victory, Mankind leaves to procure seed, but promises to return.

Dressed like a devil and carrying a net, Titivillus joins the three minions and promises that he will take revenge on Mankind for his conversion to virtue and for beating off the vices. Mankind returns and commences his labors, but becomes disgusted with his digging because a board has maliciously been placed underneath the ground to impede his efforts. He decides to rest, and, while asleep, Mischief tells him that Mercy has stolen a horse and has been hanged for his crime. Reasoning that if his virtuous mentor has thus sinned it is useless for him to continue in godly ways, Mankind resolves to give himself up to drinking and wenching. Nought, New-guise, and Nowadays return from a trip on which Titivillus had previously sent them and tell of their adventures. Mankind seeks a reconciliation with Nought, New-guise, and Nowadyas, makes a symbolic change of clothes, and resolves to steal, kill, and to give up going to church. Mercy, lamenting Mankind's fall from grace, tries to find him, but Mischief and the others confuse the search. When Mankind is finally brought forth, he fears that it is too late for a return to grace. After a suitable exhortation based on the words of Christ "Go and sin no more," and on the World, the Flesh, and the Devil, Mankind is saved. The play ends with an entreaty delivered by Mercy to the audience for self-examination and a wish for salvation for all.

Comments

This early morality is among the most humorous of all the

moralities. The five evil characters are all comic rogues, and
evey Mercy and Mankind require the skill of good comic
actors. Although in reality a devil (he signifies "the Fend of
Hell"), Titivillus, who appears also in *The Townly Plays* (ed.
George England, *EETS,* Extra Series, 1xi, 1897), is one of the
first "Vice" figures. Mercy, usually portrayed as feminine, is
here a masculine character.

See Debate of the Heavenly Graces, Appendix III. See
Hickscorner (No. XVI), *Mundus et Infans* (No. XXXVII), and
Youth (No. LIX) for three other moralities concerned with
disrespectful youth.

Critical Studies

Baker, Donald C. "The Date of *Mankind." PQ,* 42:90-91
(1963).

Brown, Arthur. "Folklore Elements in the Medieval Drama."
Folklore, 63:65-78 (1952).

Coogan, Sister Mary. *An Interpretation of the Moral Play
Mankind.* Washington, D. C.: Catholic University Press,
1947.

Fifield, Merle. *The Castle in the Circle.* Ball State Monograph
6. Muncie, Ind.: Ball State University Press, 1967. [Staging
of *Pride of Life* (No. XLIII), *Wisdom Who is Christ* (No.
LVII), *Mankind,* and *Everyman* (No. XII).]

Jones, Claude. "Walsyngham Wystyll." *JEGP,* 35:139 (1936).

Keiller, M. M. "Influence of *Piers Plowman* on the Macro
Play of *Mankind." PMLA,* 26:339-355 (1911).

MacKenzie, W. R. "New Source for *Mankind." PMLA,*
27:98-105 (1912).

Smart, W. K. *"Mankind* and the Mumming Plays." *MLN,*
32:21-25 (1917).

_____ "Some Notes on *Mankind." MP,* 14:45-58,
293-313 (1916).

XXXIII. MARRIAGE OF WIT AND SCIENCE, 1568-70
(Anonymous)

A new and Pleasant enterlude intituled the mariage of Witte and Science. Thomas Marsh, n.d.

Editions
Dodsley, II.
*Farmer, 1908.
Arthur Brown. *MSR,* 1961.

Dramatis Personae

Nature	Study
Wit	Diligence
Will	Tediousness
Reason	Recreation
Experience	Idleness
Science	Ignorance
Instruction	Shame

Length of the play: 1,547 lines.

Plot Summary
In general, the plot of the *Marriage of Wit and Science* is the same as that of Redford's *Wit and Science* (No. LVIII).

Comments
The *Marriage of Wit and Science* is dramatically inferior to the mother play *Wit and Science.* The character Will is not found in the original. Like *Wit and Science,* the *Marriage of Wit and Science* is an educational or "youth" morality (See No. LVIII).

Critical Studies
Habicht, Werner. "The Wit-Interludes and the Form of Pre-Shakespearean 'Romantic Comedy'." *RenD,* 8:73-88 (1965).

Tompkins, Kenneth D. "The Wit Plays: Variations on a
Tudor Dramatic Theme." *DA*, 28:3651A (1968).
Varma. R. S. "Act and Scene Divisions in *The Marriage of Wit
and Science.*" *N&Q*, 10:95-96 (1963).
_____ "Philosophical and Moral Ideas in *The Marriage of
Wit and Science.*" *PQ*, 44:120-122 (1965).
Withington, Robert. "Experience the Mother of Science."
PMLA, 57:592 (1942).

XXIV. MARRIAGE OF WIT AND WISDOM, c. 1570
(Francis Merbury?)

*The Contract of a Mariage betweene Wit and Wisdome very
frutefull and mixed full of pleasant mirth as well for the be-
holders as the readers or hearers, never before imprinted,*
1579. No known printer, the above title was given by the
Shakespeare Society in 1846.

Editions
Dodsley, II.
*Farmer, 1908.

Dramatis Personae
    The division of the parts for six to play this interlude:

The Prologue ⎫
Idleness   ⎬   for one
Epilogue   ⎭

Severity
Irksomeness ⎫
Snatch   ⎬   for one
Honest Recreation ⎭

Indulgence	⎫	
Wisdom	⎬ for one	
Mother Bee	⎭	
Wantonness	⎫	
Fancy	⎬ for one	
Doll	⎭	
Wit	⎫	
Search	⎬ for one	
Inquisition	⎭	
Good Nurture	⎫	
Catch	⎬ for one	
Lob	⎭	

Length of the play: 1,290 lines.

Plot Summary

Severity and his wife Indulgence admonish their son Wit, who desires to wed Wisdom. Their advice to the young man is both positive and negative — seek virtue and knowledge, but avoid Idleness and Irksomeness. Wit becomes the victim of Idleness (alias Honest Recreation) and Wantonness (Alias Mistress Modest Mirth), who not only put him to sleep, but blacken his face, take his money, and set a fool's hat on his head. Good Nurture finds the youth and delivers him to the real Honest Recreation.

Idleness himself is the victim of Snatch and Catch, two pranksters, who tie him up and steal his purse. In the company of Honest Recreation, Wit shows more charity than experience when he finds and liberates Idleness posing as Due Disport. Once again in control of the youth, Idleness brings Wit to the den of Irksomeness, who gives the newcomer a beating. With the Sword of Perseverance given him by Wisdom, Wit retorts to the beating by decapitating Irksomeness.

Once again Idleness is robbed of his money, this time by a rogue called Search. Later, Idleness makes off with a porridge

pot around his neck. Apprehended by Inquisition and identi-
fied by Mother Bee, Idleness is to be sent before the Justice.
Fancy, posing as a messenger from Wisdom, takes Wit captive,
but he is freed by Good Nurture, who announces that the
wedding of Wit and Wisdom will take place the next day.
Dressed as a priest, Idleness realizes that he will lose control
of Wit at the wedding, but consoles himself that he will still
find a clientele among the women of the world. Severity
announces the wedding of Wit to Wisdom.

Comments
    Like the other "Wit" plays, the *Marriage of Wit and Wis-
dom* is much influenced by courtly love and chivalry. It
offers proper instruction to young adults.
    Other "youth" plays:
        Glass of Government (No. XIII).
        Hickscorner (No. XVI).
        Lusty Juventus (No. XXX).
        Misogonus (No. XXXVI).
        Nice Wanton (No. XLI).
        Wit and Science (No. LVIII).
        Youth (No. LIX).
    See the other "Wit" plays:
        Marriage of Wit and Science (No. XXXIII).
        Wit and Science (No. LVIII).

Critical Studies
Greg, W. W. "The Date of *Wit and Wisdom.*" *PQ,* 11:410
    (1932).
Habicht, Werner. "The Wit Interludes and the Form of Pre-
    Shakespearean 'Romantic Comedy'." *RenD,* 8:73-88
    (1965).
Tannenbaum, Samuel A. "Comments on *The Marriage of Wit
    and Wisdom.*" *PQ,* 9:321-340 (1930).
―――――. "Dr. Tannenbaum Replies." *PQ,* 12:88-89 (1933).

Tilley, Morris. "Notes on *The Marriage of Wit and Wisdom.*"
    SAB, 10:45-57, 89-94 (1935).
Tompkins, Kenneth D. "The Wit Plays: Variations on a
    Tudor Dramatic Theme." *DA,* 28:3651A (1968).

XXXV. MARY MAGDALENE, 1480-90
(Anonymous)

Digby MS. 133.

Editions
T. Sharp. *Ancient Mysteries from the Digby Manuscript.*
    Abbotsford Club. Edinburgh, 1835.
*F. J. Furnivall. *EETS,* Extra Series, lxx, London, 1896
    (Reprinted in 1967).
Adams (first part only).

Dramatis Personae
(Only those characters that appear in the morality section
of the play are included.)
Cyrus, father of Mary Magdalene
Lazarus
Mary Magdalene } children of Cyrus
Martha
The World
Pride
Covetise
Flesh
Luxuria (Lechery)
Gluttony

Sloth
Satan
Wrath
Envy
Messenger (Sensuality)
Bad Angel
Taverner
Curiosity, a Gallant
Devil
Good Angel
Simon
Jesus
Second Devil (Belfagour)
Third Devil (Belzabub)
Spiritus Malignus

Length of the play: The entire mystery is 2,144 lines long; the morality elements constitute some 493 lines. They are 11. 49-113, 305-571, 588-747.

Plot Summary
(The following is a summary of the morality segments only, that is, Part I, Scenes 2, 7-11, 13-15.

Cyrus, the Lord of Jerusalem, the Castle of Maudleyn, and Bethany, announces his will in favor of his three children. Lazarus will inherit Jerusalem, Mary will receive the Castle of Maudleyn, and Martha will possess Bethany. The World, the Flesh, and the Devil reveal themselves in self-descriptive monologues. Pride and Covetise serve World; Lechery, Gluttony, and Sloth follow Flesh; Wrath and Envy are the minions of the Devil. The three Evil Powers congregate in the tent of World and plot Mary's downfall. The Seven Deadly Sins begin a siege of the Castle of Maudleyn, but then depart for Jerusalem. Lechery and Bad Angel enter to tempt Mary, who is still in mourning for her deceased father. Sympathetic to the persuasive words of the vice, she agrees to go to

99

Jerusalem where she abandons herself to a gallant named
Curiosity. Lechery is commanded by the Devil to keep Mary
in sin. Rejoicing in their success, the three Evil Powers take
leave of one another. Good Angel warns Mary in her sleep to
take care of her sinful soul now destined for hell. She bemoans her sins and resolves to follow Christ, whom she finds
at a banquet given by Simon. Mary washes his feet and in
turn receives forgiveness for her sins. The Bad Angel is
punished by the two devils Belfagour and Belzabub, and the
Seven Deadly Sins are exorcized from Mary. Devils set the
house on fire and Mary returns to her family.

Comments
The Digby *Mary Magdalene* is obviously a unique play; it is
the only English mystery containing a morality.

Critical Studies
Bowers, Robert H. "The Tavern Scene in the Middle English
Digby Play of *Mary Magdalene.*" In *All These to Teach:
Essays in Honor of C. A. Robertson.* Ed. A. Bryan et al.
Gainesville: University of Florida Press (1965), pp. 15-32.

Hoffmann, M. N. *Die Magdalenenszenen im geistlichen Spiel
des deutschen Mittelalters.* Wursburg: Konrad Triltsch,
1933.

Knoll, Friedrich Otto. *Die Rolle der Maria Magdalena im
geistlichen Spiel des Mittelalters.* Berlin and Leipsig:
W. de Gruyter, 1934.

Lewis, Leon Eugene. "The Play of Mary Magdalene." *DA,*
23:4685-4686 (1963).

Ritchie, Harry. "A Suggested Location for the Digby *Mary
Magdalene.*" *ThS,* 4:51-58 (1963).

Schmidt, Karl. "Die Digby-Spiele." *Anglia,* 8:371-404
(1885).

XXXVI. MISOGONUS, 1560-77
(Laurentius Bariona?)

A mery and p[leasaunt comedie called?] Misogonus...
Laurentius Bariona. Kettheringe. Die 20 Novembris, Anno
1577. The Prologue is followed by the signature Thomas
Rychardes.

Editions
Brandl.
*Farmer, 1906.
R. W. Bond. *Early Plays from the Italian.* Oxford, 1911.

Dramatis Personae
  Prologue
  Philogonus, pater
  Eupelas, fidelis patris vicinus (faithful friend of Philogonus)
  Cacurgus, morio (fool)
  Misogonus, filius domesticus (son living at home)
  Orgelus, servus Misogoni (servant of Misogonus)
  OEnophilus, conservus eius (fellow servant)
  Liturgus, servus Philogoni (servant of Philogonus)
  Melissa, meretrix (prostitute)
  Sir John, sacredos (priest)
  Jack, clarke
  Ceister Codrus, rusticus (a rustic)
  Alison, eius uxor, obstetrix (his wife, a midwife)
  Isbell Busbey
  Madge Caro   testes vetulae (old women witnesses)
  Eugonus, filius peregrinus (lost son)
  Crito, peregrinus (traveler)
  Epilogus

Length of the fragment: approximately 1,950 lines.

101

Plot Summary

Philogonus, the unhappy parent of a spoiled and already corrupt Misogonus, accepts the help of his friend Eupelas, who offers to attempt the conversion of the young profligate. The supposed fool Cacurgus (in reality the Vice of the play) overhears their conversation and resolves to inform Misogonus of their desire to reform him. The forewarned Misogonus proves to Eupelas that he is not to be converted by giving the older man a good beating. Philogonus hears of this disgraceful conduct through his servant Liturgus and regrets his indulgence in rearing Misogonus. In the next scenes are introduced the wayward friends of Misogonus, who demonstrate their skills at drinking, dancing, and whoring. Melissa is the prostitute, and the gambling is supervised by the worldly priest Sir John. Philogonus, Eupelas, and Liturgus break in on the festivities, but are unable to curtail them. Later, Philogonus learns that he has another son. This discovery enables him to disinherit Misogonus in favor of the new-found Eugonus, who is as good as Misogonus is bad. Although Misogonus is disinherited, he is on the verge of reconciliation when the fragment ends.

Comments

Although the scene is Laurentius in Italy and the style is that of Roman comedy imitating the *Acolastus, Misogonus* is English in spirit. There is much of the farce in *Misogonus;* it belongs, however, to the education or "youth" moralities and is probably a school play. *Misogonus* resembles many of the continental pieces based on the popular theme of the prodigal son. The author's name has been convincingly shown to be Laurence Johnson.

Other "youth" plays:
>*Glass of Government* (No. XIII).
>*Hickscorner* (No. XVI).
>*Lusty Juventus* (No. XXX).
>*Marriage of Wit and Wisdom* (No. XXXIV).

Nice Wanton (No. XLI).
Wit and Science (No. LVIII).
Youth (No. LIX).

Critical Studies
Barber, Lester E. *"Misogonus:* Edited with an Introduction."
  DA, 28:1046A (1967).
Bevington, David. *"Misogonus* and Laurentius Bariona."
  ELN, 2:9-10 (1965).
Kittredge, G. L. "The *Misogonus* and Laurence Johnson."
  JEGP, 3:335-341 (1901).
Tannenbaum, Samuel. "A Note on *Misogonus." MLN,*
  45:308-310 (1930).

XXXVII. MUNDUS ET INFANS, 1500-20
(Anonymous)

Here begynneth a propre newe Interlude of the Worlde and the chylde, otherwyse called Mundus & Infans & it sheweth of the estate of Chyldehode and Manhode. Wynkyn de Worde, 1522.

Editions
Dodsley, I.
Manly, I.
*Farmer, 1905.

Dramatis Personae
   Mundus (World)
   Infans (also Wanton, Lust and Liking, Manhood, Shame,
      Age, and Repentance)
   Conscience
   Folly
   Perseverance

Length of the play: 979 lines.

Plot Summary
   Mundus introduces himself as a "Prince of Power" and
commands obedience from all. The newly born Infans immediately enters the service of Mundus, who gives him fine
clothes and confers on him the name of Wanton. After boasting of pranks revealing him to be a thoroughly spoiled child,
Wanton reaches his fourteenth year and is given the new name
of Lust and Liking. A few lines of commentary bring the
young Lust and Liking through seven years of rollicking fun,
and, at the age of twenty-one, he receives yet another name,
Manhood. Mundus tells Manhood of the Seven Deadly Sins
and dubs him knight. Arrogantly aware of his supposed
excellence, Manhood meets Conscience from whom he receives a warning against Pride and the other Deadly Sins to
whom he has already vowed allegiance. Only Covetise is not
condemned because, according to Conscience, it is good to
covet the right things. Moderation is important, but the best
advice Conscience can give is to beware of false and flattering
Folly, a composite of the Deadly Sins. Left to himself, the
converted Manhood speaks a monologue promising to follow
the true teaching of Conscience. Folly noisily enters, and,
with a flood of indecent language, accosts Manhood and
finally persuades him to travel to London for a good time in
the stews. Using the pseudonym of Shame to escape detec-
tion, Manhood is about to follow Folly when Conscience
enters with a plea to remain. Heedless of Conscience,

Manhood goes to London. While he engages in a life of sin, Conscience and Perseverance lament Manhood's fall from grace. Corrupted by sin, Manhood returns under the name of Age. He regrets the day he was born and his past life. Perseverance saves him from despair and re-converts Manhood, who takes the name of Repentance.

Comments

Mundus et Infans is a shortened "full-scope" morality, i.e. it is allegorical in structure, and has as its dramatis personae personified abstractions or universalized types, and is primarily concerned with man's salvation, presenting in visible terms and according to Christian teaching the moral conflict experienced by each and every man through his entire life on earth. The fact that only two actors were used to present the play necessitates much economy in its production. Folly, therefore, represents all the Deadly Sins and Mundus is the only Evil Power (the World, the Flesh, and the Devil) to have an active role.

See *Hickscorner* (No. XVI), *Mankind* (No. XXXII), and *Youth* (No. LIX) for three other early moralities concerned with disrespectful youth. See also the *Castle of Perseverance* (No. V), the finest extant example of the "full-scope" morality.

Critical Studies

MacCracken, H. N. "A Source of *Mundus et Infans.*" *PMLA*, 23:486-496 (1908).

XXXVIII. NATURE, 1490-1501
(Henry Medwall)

A goodly interlude of Nature compyled by mayster Henry Medwall chapleyn to the ryght reuerent father in god Iohan Morton sometyme Cardynall and Archebyshop of Canterbury. Folio, no date, printed c. 1520.

Editions
Brandl.
*Farmer, 1907.

Dramatis Personae

Nature	Wrath	Chastity
Man	Envy	Good Occupation
Reason	Sloth	Shamefacedness
Sensuality	Gluttony	Mundus (World)
Innocency	Humility	Patience
Worldly Affection	Charity	Pride
Bodily Lust	Abstinence	
	Liberality	
	Garcon (boy)	

Length of the play: approximately 2,700 lines.

Plot Summary
    As God's representative on earth, Nature gives serious advice to inexperienced Man, who is about to begin life's awesome journey. Along with Innocence, Man's companions will be Sensuality and Reason, the latter hopefully acting as leader. Sensuality immediately challenges the supremacy of Reason while confused Man silently stands in the background. World easily persuades Man to abandon Innocency and to employ as servants Worldly Affection, the wronged Sensuality, and Pride. Having delivered an entertaining functional description of his own ostentatious garments, Pride (alias

106

Worship) influences Man to dress in the latest fashion and to frequent Pride's friends. Man's break with Reason is reported to the audience by Sensuality and Worldly Affection:

> My master . . .
> Drew out his sword without more tarrying
> And smote Reason on the head,
> That I have great marvel but he be now dead.

By now well initiated into a life of sin, Man has become familiar with whores — Margery in particular — and has entertained Envy (Disdain), Wrath (Manhood), Gluttony (Good Fellowship), Covetise (Wordly Policy), Sloth (Ease), and Leachery (Lust), all kinsmen of Worldly Affection. Only Covetise, the sin of old age, is neglected by the still youthful Man. Seeming to regret his sinful deeds, Man dismisses Worldly Affection and Sensuality, and is reconciled temporarily to Reason.

Reason begins Part II with a comparison of the life of man to a siege of a castle (See Psychomachia, Appendix V). Three days have gone by since Man's return to grace, and, as he points out to Sensuality, he has not had a bit of fun all the while. Bodily Lust interests Man in a new whore and Worldly Affection offers to console Margery in Man's absence. When the plans of Bodily Lust miscarry, they seek out in the stews the services of the always available Margery, who, unfortunately, never appears on stage. A pitched combat between the Vices and the Virtues is prepared, but never materializes. Man has now become the victim of Age, and, to the dismay of the Vices, frequents Reason. Only Covetise is in favor with Man. Reason prevails upon Man to repent his sins. Seven Virtues each offer proper instruction to Man in the dispelling of the seven vices — Meekness-Pride, Charity-Envy, Patience-Wrath, Good Occupation-Sloth, Liberality-Avarice, Abstinence-Gluttony, Chastity-Lechery. The play ends with a final reconciliation between Man and Reason.

Comments

Nature is an early morality occupying a pivotal position between the medieval homiletic drama and the secularized Tudor and Elizabethan drama. The characters are cast according to humanistic principles, but the scope and conflict of the play is in accordance with the earlier morality theater.

See *The Castle of Perseverance* (No. V) for the finest extant example of the "full-scope" morality; also, *Nature of the Four Elements* (No. XXXIX), a play based on *Nature* in many ways.

Critical Studies

Moeslein, Mary E. "A Critical Edition of the Plays of Henry Medwall." *DA*, 29:2270A (1969).

MacKenzie, W. R. "Source for Medwall's *Nature.*" *PMLA*, 29:189-199 (1914).

XXXIX. NATURE OF THE FOUR ELEMENTS, 1517-18
(John Rastell)

A new interlude and a mery of the nature of the iiij elements declarynge many proper poyntes of phylosophy naturall, and of dyuers straunge landys, and of dyuers straunge effectes & causes, whiche interlude yf the hole matter be playd wyl conteyne the space of an hour and a halfe, but yf ye lyst ye may leue out muche of the sad mater as the messengers parte, and some of naturys parte and some of experyens parte and yet the matter wyl depend conuenyently, and than it wyll not be paste thre quarters of an hour of length. No date, the only surviving copy is imperfect.

Editions
J. O. Halliwell. Percy Society, XXII (1848).
Dodsley, I.
J. Fisher. *Marburger Studien,* V (1903).
*Farmer, 1905.

Dramatis Personae

The Messenger	Sensual Appetite
Nature	The Taverner
Humanity	Experience
Studious Desire	Ignorance

also, if ye list, ye may bring in a Disguising.

Here follow divers matters which be in this interlude contained.

Of the situation of the four elements, that is to say, the earth, the water, the air, and the fire, and of their qualities and properties, and of the generation and corruption of things made of the commixtion of them.

Of certain conclusions proving that the earth must needs be round, and that it hangeth in the midst of the firmament, and that it is in circumference above 21,000 miles.

Of certain conclusions proving that the sea lieth round upon the earth.

Of certain points of cosmography, as how and where the sea covereth the earth, and of divers strange regions and lands, and which way they lie; and of the newfound lands and the manner of the people.

Of the generation and cause of stone and metal, and of plants and herbs.

Of the generation and cause of well-springs and rivers; and of the cause of hot fumes that come out of the earth; and of the cause of the baths of water in the earth, which be perpetually hot.

Of the cause of the ebb and flood of the sea.

Of the cause of rain, snow, and hail.

Of the cause of the winds and thunder.

XXXIX

Of the cause of the lightning, of blazing stars, and flames flying in the air.

Length of the fragment: 1,457 lines.

Plot Summary

The opening speech of the Messenger is excessively long, but contains many interesting points. We learn that the playwright, although of little skill, desires to treat of some matters of natural philosophy. It is time, he says through his Messenger, that something worth hearing be written in English. The Greeks and Romans possessed excellent works in their mother tongues, and there is no reason why learned clerks should not take the pains to produce "works of gravity" in English, especially, the Messenger adds, since English is now capable of saying almost anything. Furthermore, because there are many nobles and commoners who do not understand Latin, the author opts for all writing and learning to be henceforth in English. He also reasons that if every semi-learned clerk in the land can try his hand at writing, he can too. A main point of the prologue is the condemnation of those who work only to gain riches for themselves without thinking of the good of the nation. Finally, the Messenger proposes putting first things first, but in a way suitable to the new view of the cosmos. How, he argues, can learned men dispute profound and abstract theological matters when they know nothing of the visible manifestations of nature? It is much more logical to proceed from the knowledge of earthly things to an understanding of God, than to deal immediately and exclusively with remote matters of theology. Thus, the interlude to be presented will concern itself with the four elements and other scientific phenomena. The Messenger consoles the less inquisitive and erudite of the audience with the assurance that there will be no rhetoric or difficult language and much merry jesting.

Nature, the special minister of God, Humanity, and

110

Studious Desire enter. Addressing himself to Humanity,
Nature convinces Humanity that to know God one must
know his creatures first:

> But man to know God is a difficulty
> Except by a mean he himself inure,
> Which is to know God's creatures that be.

Having established this sensible approach to the acquisition
of divine knowledge, Nature subjects the grateful Humanity
to detailed instruction in medieval and Renaissance cosmol-
ogy and physics, some of which seems strikingly modern (for
example, the indestructibility of matter). Studious Desire is
left with Humanity as an incentive to the acquisition of more
science.

When Humanity admits that he did not understand the
arguments of Nature concerning the global shape of the earth,
Studious Desire explains the fact to him with pertinent examples. Because Humanity still does not quite understand
this point, Studious Desire offers to search for Experience,
who, with the help of scientific instruments, is able to make
all men understand.

Sensual Appetite rudely interrupts them, but makes a
significant point: that he, Sensual Appetite, is absolutely
necessary for man and shares in the approval of Nature.
When, at Humanity's request, Studious Desire leaves the
stage, Sensual Appetite brings Humanity to a tavern for recreation; here is fulfilled the author's promise of comic relief.
At the tavern they plan festivities at which will be "little
Nell," "Jane with the black lace," and "bouncing Bess." It is
unfortunate that they never appear on stage.

When Sensual Appetite and Humanity leave the stage to
begin their merrymaking, Experience and Studious Desire
begin an interesting lesson on world geography based on the
recent voyages of Experience. Sensual Appetite and Humanity join Experience and Studious Desire, but Sensual Appetite
leaves the company after failing a spelling test designed to
demonstrate his inability to learn. Humanity is now able to

XXXIX

ask Experience questions Studious Desire could not answer
properly. Experience then proves that the earth is spherical
by two examples and also begins to demonstrate his scientific
instruments. (Eight leaves of text are here missing.) The play
resumes with a short self-description by a new character,
Ignorance. Sensual Appetite speaks of a recent skirmish (possibly occurring in the eight missing leaves) in which he re-
pelled "the 'losophers." Ignorance and Sensual Appetite
come upon Humanity, who is now exhausted after his learning experiences, and convince him that learning only leads to
madness. They entertain a group of revelers in singing and
dancing. Nature enters and admonishes Humanity, who
maintains that both Sensual Appetite and Studious Desire
are necessary to man. Nature responds that they are truly
both necessary, but that one must not put all one's delight in
things sensual. A proper subservience of the flesh to the spirit
is necessary:

> Though it be for thee full necessary
> For thy comfort sometime to satisfy
> Thy sensual appetite,
> Yet it is not convenient for thee
> To put therein thy felicity
> And all thy whole delight.

The play ends here imperfectly.

Comments

Nature of the Four Elements is a product of Christian
humanism and is closely related to Medwall's earlier play
Nature (No. XXXVIII). The relationship between Rastell and
the More circle should also be noted. Significant is the
portrayal of the character Nature as masculine. There is some
philosophical confusion on Rastell's part concerning the
character Nature. Pearl Hogrefe in *The Sir Thomas More
Circle,* pp. 265-66 adequately explains Rastell's use of Nature
Naturate, Natura Naturata, and Nature naturans. Experience
is a new character on the morality stage; Ignorance is the

Vice. The only principle of organization in *Nature of the Four Elements* is that of alternation: the sober scenes of instruction are interspersed with those of merrymaking.

Critical Studies
Baskervill, C. R. "John Rastell's Dramatic Activities." *MP*, 13:557-560 (1916).
Borish, M. E. "Source and Intention of *The Four Elements.*" *SP*, 35:149-163 (1938).
Greg, W. W. "Notes on Some Early Plays. . .Rastell's *Nature of the Four Elements,* Printer and Date. . ." *The Library*, Ser.4, 11:44-56 (1930).
Nugent, Elizabeth. "Sources of Rastell's *Four Elements.*" *PMLA*, 57:74-88 (1942).
Parks, George B. "The Geography of the *Interlude of the Four Elements.*" *PQ*, 17:251-262 (1938).
Parr, Johnstone. "More Sources of Rastell's *Interlude of the Four Elements.*" *PMLA*, 60:48-58 (1945).
Stelle, Robert. "A Note on *A New Interlude.*" *The Library*, Ser.4, 9:90-91 (1928).

XL. NEW CUSTOM, 1559-73
(Anonymous)

A new Enterlude No less wittie: then pleasant, entituled new Custome, deuised of late, and for diuerse causes nowe set forthe, neuer before this tyme Imprinted. William How for Abraham Veale, 1573.

Editions
Dodsley, III.
*Farmer, 1906.

Dramatis Personae
 Four may easily play this Interlude:
Perverse Doctrine, an old Popish Priest
Ignorance   ⎫
Hypocrisy   ⎬   2
and Edification ⎭
New Custom, a Minister ⎫
Avarice, a Ruffler (Bully)⎬ 3
Assurance, a Virtue ⎭
Light of the Gospel   ⎫
Cruelty, a Ruffler (Bully)⎪
God's Felicity   ⎬ 4
The Prologue   ⎭

Length of the play: 1,076 lines.

Plot Summary
 The Prologue denounces those who say that the reformed religion is to be called New Custom when it is in reality the true religion as instituted by Christ and free from later (Catholic) corruptions. Perverse Doctrine and Ignorance marvel that so many young people now fancy themselves theologians and talk nothing but Scripture. Especially concerned about a new preacher named New Custom, they resolve to "use the Villain" with him. To assure success, Perverse Doctrine will use the alias Sound Doctrine, and Ignorance will be called Simplicity. New Custom bemoans the fact that sin is now taken so lightly and actually passes before the world as virtue. Confronting Perverse Doctrine, New Custom maintains that he is not New Custom at all but Primitive Constitution, the true, original, and uncorrupted Christianity. When Perverse Doctrine decides it best to call on his sister Hypocrisy for help, New Custom receives corresponding support from Light of the Gospel, who suggests that they confront once again Perverse Doctrine and Ignorance. The vices are alarmed that Light of the Gospel is in England and resolve to discuss

114

the matter with Cruelty and his companion Avarice. After
some typical lines of self-description, the two new vices adopt
the aliases of Justice with Severity and Frugality and join
forces with Perverse Doctrine and Ignorance. Perverse Doctrine first confronts Light of the Gospel, but cannot resist the
virtue and is converted. He now becomes Sincere Doctrine
and recognizes New Custom as Primitive Constitution. Edification, Assurance, and God's Felicity enter as companions of
Light of the Gospel. The play ends with a prayer that Queen
Elizabeth may always work for the good of the people.

Comments
New Custom is a Protestant morality, but not one of bitter
hatred for Catholics. The play's purpose is the conversion not
the extermination of Catholics.
Other Protestant plays:
> *Conflict of Conscience* (No. IX).
> *King Darius* (No. XXI).
> *King John* (No. XXII).
> *Three Laws* (No. XLIX).

Critical Studies
Baskervill, C. R. "On Two Old Plays." *MP,* 14:16 (1916).
Feuillerat, Albert. "An Unknown Protestant Morality Play."
    MLR, 9:94-96 (1914).
Oliver, Leslie. "John Foxe and the Drama *New Custom."*
    HLQ, 10:407-410 (1947).

XLI. NICE WANTON, 1547-53
(Anonymous)

A Preaty Interlude called, Nice Wanton. John King, 1560.

Editions
Dodsley, II.
*Manly, I.
Farmer, 1905.

Dramatis Personae

The Messenger	Iniquity
Barnabas	Baily Errand (Bailiff)
Ismael	Xantipe
Dalila	Worldly Shame
Eulalia	Daniel, the Judge

Length of the play: 552 lines.

Plot Summary

Nice Wanton is the story of Barnabas, Ismael, and Dalila, the three children of the overindulgent mother Xantippe. Barnabas is a good son and student, whereas, when the play begins, Dalila and Ismael are already master juvenile delinquents. Their neighbor Eulalia, tired of the bad example of Dalila and Ismael, tries to no avail to persuade Xantippe that strong discipline at home can only help the two youngsters. With the help of Iniquity, the Vice, Dalila and Ismael enter eagerly on the broad road to perdition. Their bawdy life in sin appears in song, swearing, a long game of dice, and bawdy conversation. The stage direction calls for a "long interval," which is meant to indicate the passage of time from youthful folly to hardened crime and immorality. Dalila enters crooked, lame, and starving. She is pock-marked and bald — a certain indication of venereal disease. Her good brother Barnabas brings her words of comfort and forgiveness, and

116

they depart. Judge Daniel, Iniquity, and the Bailiff enter for the trial of Ismael, who has been accused of felony, burglary, and murder. Iniquity appears as a witness against him, and the death penalty is invoked. Having announced the death of Dalila and the hanging of Ismael, Worldly Shame searches for Xantippe that he may taunt her with their deaths. Xantippe is so stricken with grief that she is about to take her own life when Barnabas also offers her forgiveness from God. The play ends with a final repetition of the moral of the play: "He that spareth the rod, the chyld doth hate."

Comments

Nice Wanton, a school play, is an educational or "youth" morality similar to many continental pieces. It is the first English morality that verges on tragedy and the first with bifurcated Mankind figures.

Other "youth" plays:

> *Glass of Government* (No. XIII).
> *Hickscorner* (No. XVI).
> *Lusty Juventus* (No. XXX).
> *Marriage of Wit and Wisdom* (No. XXXIV).
> *Misogonus* (No. XXXVI).
> *Wit and Science* (No. LVIII).
> *Youth,* (No. LIX).

Other plays with a bifurcated Mankind figure:

> *Enough is as Good as a Feast* (No. XI).
> *Glass of Government* (No. XIII).
> *Like Will to Like* (No. XXV).
> *Tide Tarrieth No Man* (No. LI).
> *Trial of Treasure* (No. LIII).

See Coming of Death (Appendix I).

XLII. PATIENT AND MEEK GRISSILL, 1561-65
(John Phillip)

The Commodye of patient and meeke Grissill, Whearin is declared, the good example, of her pacience towardes her husband: and lykewise, the due obedience of Children, toward their Parents. Newly Compiled by Iohn Philip. Thomas Colwell, n.d.

Edition
W. W. Greg and R. B. McKerrow. *MSR,* 1909.

Dramatis Personae
Politic Persuasion, the Vice
Gautier, Marquis of Salutia
Fidence ⎫
Reason ⎬   courtiers
Sobriety ⎭
Grissill, daughter to Janicle
The Mother of Grissill
Janicle, a peasant
Indigent Poverty, his friend
Two Lackeys
[Ladies of the Court]
Diligence, messenger of Gautier
Nurse of Grissill's children
[Maid to Grissill]
Countess of Pango, sister to Gautier
Maid to the Countess
A Midwife
Rumor
Vulgus, a citizen of Salutia
Patience
Constancy
Daughter ⎫
Son   ⎬   of Grissill

(On the title page these characters are listed in order of appearance, but the Ladies of the Court and Grissill's Maid are omitted. A character named Sansper is called upon to enter but never speaks, (1. 58). This may be another name for Fidence — Sans Peur. See *MSR*, Introd., p. xiii-xiv.)

Length of the play: 2,141 lines.

Plot Summary

Having joined the hunting party of the Marquis Gautier, the Vice Politic Persuasion overhears Gautier's companions Fidence, Reason, and Sobriety urge their master to wed, but with the stipulation that no one will oppose his choice of bride. The scene changes to introduce Grissill, her moribund mother, her father Janicle, and a neighbor named Indigence, who serves to point out the extreme poverty of Grissill's family. While the court waits impatiently for Gautier to reveal the name of the next countess, Grissill's mother dies leaving her faithful daughter to care for Janicle. Gautier's choice falls on Grissill, who, once the paternal consent is won, marries her lord.

Now a regular standby at court, Politic Persuasion vows to cause much trouble for Grissill. He sees his first chance upon hearing Gautier sing the praises of Grissill's excellence, and suggests to him that her virtues would soon fall away if she were tested. Gautier readily agrees to test Grissill, and, as a first tribulation, tells his wife that the nobles have demanded his exile or the life of their child. Diligence feigns the child's murder, but in reality delivers the baby into the care of Gautier's aunt, the Countess of Pango. True to the words of the Prologue commending her moral integrity, Grissill bears her grief virtuously. She next gives birth to a son, who is apparently murdered, but also, like his sister, sent off to the Countess of Pango. A third tribulation sends Grissell home to her father to allow Gautier to chose a wife of his own class. True to form, unfortunate Grissill bears her repudiation like

119

the saint she is. Realizing the dauntless persistence in virtue of Grissill and his own plan thereby thwarted, Politic Persuasion bids farewell to the court. Patience and Constancy make brief appearances in witness to Grissill's virtue.

The final trial calls Grissill forth to prepare the festivities for the wedding of Count Gautier, and, in particular, to concern herself with the comfort of the new bride. The time to reveal all has come. Gautier's new countess is, of course, nonexistent and the two children are brought forth and reunited to their father and mother. Grissill's patience and meekness are declared unparalleled, and are held up as an example for all. The Epilogue consists of a prayer worthy of any Elizabethan divine that Queen Elizabeth and her council may work for the good of the commonweal.

Comments

Patient and Meek Grissill is a hybrid "virtue" play. Except for the Vice Politic Persuasion, there are no genuine allegorical figures in the play. The three companions Fidence, Reason, and Sobriety are human in every respect but their names. The setting of the play is Salutia. The plot was, of course, a popular one in the Middle Ages and the Renaissance.

Other "virtue" plays:

> *Appius and Virginia* (No. III).
> *Godly Queen Hester* (No. XIV).
> *Life and Repentance of Mary Magdalene* (No. XXIV).
> *Virtuous and Godly Susanna* (No. LIV).

Critical Studies

Bang, W. "Zur *Patient Grissill.*" *Archiv,* 107:110-12 (1901).

Halstead, W. L. "Collaboration on *The Patient Grissill.*" *PQ,* 18:381-394 (1939).

Krzyzanowski, Julius. "Conjectural Remarks on Elizabethan Dramatists." *N&Q,* 195:400-402 (1950).

Roberts, Charles W. "An Edition of John Phillip's *Commodye of pacient and meeke Grisill.*" University of Illinois Dissertation, 1938.

Wright, Louis B. "A Political Reflection in Phillip's *Patient Grissel." RES,* 4:424-428 (1928).

XLIII. PRIDE OF LIFE, 1400-25
(Anonymous)

The MS., destroyed by fire in Dublin in 1922, lacked the final part of the play. *Pride of Life* was first published by Mills in 1891.

Editions
J. Mills. *Proceedings of the Royal Society of Antiquaries of Ireland.* Dublin, 1891.
Brandl.
*O. Waterhouse. *EETS,* Extra Series, civ, London, 1909.
N. Davis. *EETS,* Supplementary Texts I. London, 1970.

Dramatis Personae
    Prolocutor
    Rex Vivus, King of Life
    Fortitudo, (Strength) the First Soldier
    Sanitas, (Health) the Second Soldier
    Regina (Queen)
    Nuntius (Messenger) Mirth
    Episcopus, the Bishop

Length of the fragment: 502 lines.

Plot Summary
    Fortunately the Prologue summarizes the entire play. The

proud King of Life is surrounded by handsome knights and an educated Queen, who reminds her lord to think on indiscriminating Death. When the King persists in his pride, the Queen sends for the Bishop, who reiterates the Queen's warning. Death and the King confront each other. The Prologue ends with a reference to the propitiatory prayers of the Virgin Mary on behalf of the sinner.

The King of Life, in a manner resembling King Herod of the mystery plays, begins the action of the play boasting of his great power. Armed with weapons brought by his two knights Strength and Health, the King fears no one and expects to live always. Warned by the Queen that Death will surely strike him down, the King derives support from his two knights and from his messenger Mirth, to whom he offers the Castle of Gailispire and the Earldom of Kent. Called upon by the Queen to preach to the King, the Bishop also fails to convert his worldly lord. The king next sends Mirth to search out anyone who will dare fight him. The fragment ends as the King's challenge is extended even to the King of Death.

The Prologue permits a reconstruction of the rest of the play: the King of Life meets Death in combat and is conquered. He then possibly appears before God the Father, who, at the request of the Blessed Virgin, grants salvation to the King of Life.

Comments

Pride of Life is the earliest extant English morality, but quite distinct in character from other early moralities such as the *Castle of Perseverance* (No. V), and *Mundus et Infans* (No. XXXVII). Like *Everyman* (No. XII), it deals exclusively with approaching Death and relates to the late medieval theme of the Dance of Death.

See *Everyman* (No. XII).

Debate of the Body and Soul (Appendix II).

Coming of Death (Appendix I).

Critical Studies

Brown, Carleton. *"The Pride of Life* and the Twelve Abuses."
  Archiv, 127:72-78 (1912).
Fifield, Merle. *The Castle in the Circle.* Ball State Monograph
  6. Muncie, Ind.: Ball State University Press, 1967. [Staging
  of *Pride of Life, Wisdom Who is Christ* (No. LVII), *Man-*
  kind (No. XXXII), and *Everyman* (No. XII).]
Heuser, W. *Die Kildare-Gedichte.* Bonner Beiträge zur
  Anglistik XIV. Bonn, 1904.
Holthausen, F. *"The Pride of Life." Archiv,* 108:34-48
  (1902).
MacKenzie, William R. "The Debate over the Soul in *The*
  Pride of Life." Washington University Studies, Humanistic
  Series, 9:263-274 (1922).

XLIV. RESPUBLICA, 1553
(Anonymous)

A merye enterlude entitled Respublica, made in the yeare
of our Lorde 1553, and the first yeare of the moste prosper-
ous Reigne of our moste gracious Soveraigne, Queene Marye
the first. Macro MS.

Editions

J. P. Collier. *Illustrations of Old English Literature,* I.
  London, 1886.
Brandl.
*L. A. Magnus. *EETS,* Extra Series, xciv, London, 1905.
Farmer, 1907.
W. W. Greg. *EETS,* No. 226, London, 1952.

Dramatis Personae
The Prologue, A poet
Avarice, alias Policy, the vice of the play
Insolence, alias Authority, the chief gallant
Oppression, alias Reformation, another gallant
Adulation, alias Honesty, the third gallant
People, representing the poor Commons
Respublica, a widow
Misericordia ⎞
Veritas   ⎟   four ladies
Iusticia   ⎟
Pax   ⎠
Nemesis, the goddess of redress and correction.

Length of the play: 1,940 lines.

Plot Summary
The Prologue introduces the play as a political morality designed to demonstrate that better times are coming now that Mary I is Queen of England. Avarice enters first, declares his new alias Policy, comments on the lamentable state of Respublica (England), and states his intention of causing even more trouble. In the remaining scenes of Act I Avarice becomes the leader of other vices — Insolence, Oppression, and Adulation. He assigns them new names which they receive with varying degrees of intelligence. Insolence becomes Authority, Adulation becomes Honesty, and Oppression receives the new name of Reformation. The plan is for Avarice (Policy) to gain a position in the government and, thereby, to promote the others.

Respublica begins Act II bemoaning the constant vacillation in the affairs of state. Avarice, posing as good Policy, gains the confidence of Respublica and introduces his three minions to her. She exhorts them to stamp out the very vices they are and leaves them to themselves. The Act closes with the song "Bring ye to me and I to thee."

After a short speech declaring that she is still hopeful of better times, Respublica speaks with Adulation, who praises his own selflessness and that of his comrades. People enters and is welcomed by Respublica, but Adulation cannot understand his speech (Devonshire). People complains that the times are almost impossible: prices are steadily rising. He complains also of Flattery, Oppression, and Insolence, whose name he cannot remember. Although portrayed as uneducated and simple, People is better at character analysis than is Respublica. When she introduces Adulation as Honesty, People immediately senses the falsity of the figure before him and only with difficulty takes the word of Respublica. Respublica and People leave together as the four vices enter. Avarice is richer than ever and carries three well-filled bags of money. Oppression (Reformation) is tired of deposing bishops. Avarice scolds Adulation, who receives only £300 per annum. Avarice also confesses by what means he obtained his bags of money — bribes of office, sales of livings and church goods, filching from customs, forged wares, illegal exports, deceiving simpletons, etc. After a song Avarice advises them all to make haste because Time has a daughter Verity who babbles all. He also teaches them about the goddess Occasion, whose only hair is a forelock which must be seized before she passes by. The three minions leave, and Avarice drags his bags of money home.

Respublica begins Act IV dressed in torn and ragged clothes and is still dismayed at the dismal state of affairs. She converses with People and points out that five or six years ago (before the reign of Edward) People was prosperous. Avarice is called to task but is aided by his friends, who silence People. Mercy opens Act V with a monologue on Divine forgiveness. Respublica is grateful at Mercy's coming, but Avarice and Adulation realize that Mercy and her friend Truth must be put off. Mercy now brings in Truth, who finally convinces Respublica that her ministers have been false. Justice and Peace shall be called on to restore harmony, and Mercy will pardon the weak. Avarice attempts to take credit for the changes about to occur but Respublica repudiates him and his companions, who, after much verbal protestation, remove their disguises. Justice assigns the four vices to People. Nemesis (Queen Mary) commands Respublica and People to approach, and accuses the four vices of their respective crimes. The four virtues debate the fate of the vices. Adulation repents and receives pardon, but Oppression and Insolence must await sentencing. Avarice is to be delivered to the Head Officer. The play ends with thanks to God and praise for Queen Mary.

Comments

Respublica, performed at Christmas 1553, concerns the six years of the reign of Edward VI. The play is pro-Catholic dealing not with doctrine but with the social evils of the Reformation. The three lesser vices are, as Magnus says (*Respublica,* Introduction, p. 3), mainly clowns, Avarice being the chief Vice.

See *Impatient Poverty* (No. XVIII).
   Temperance and Humility (No. XLVII).
   Coming of Death (Appendix I).
   Debate of the Heavenly Graces (Appendix III).

Critical Studies

Bradner, Leicester. "A Test for Udall's Authorship." *MLN,* 42:378-380 (1927).

Scheurweghs, G. "The Relative Pronouns in the XVIth [Century?] Plays *Royster Doister* and *Respublica:* A Frequency Study." *ES,* 45: Supplement, 84-89 (1964).

Starr, G. A. "Notes on *Respublica.*" *N&Q,* 8:290-292 (1961).

XLV. SATIRE OF THE THREE ESTATES, 1535-40
(Sir David Lindsay)

Ane Satyre of The Thrie Estaits, in commendation of vertew and vituperation of vyce. Maid by Sir Dauid Lindsay of the Mont, alias, Lyon King of Armes. Robert Charteris, Edinburgh, 1602.

Editions
G. Chalmers. *Poetical Works of Sir David Lindsay.* London, 1806.

*F. Hall et al. *Works of Sir David Lindsay. EETS,* Old Series, xxxvii, London, 1869.

D. Laing. *Poetical Works of Sir David Lindsay.* Edinburgh, 1879.

D. Hamer. *Works of Sir David Lindsay,* II. Scottish Text Society. Edinburgh, 1931.

M. McDiarmid. *Satire of the Three Estates.* London: Heinemann Educational Books, 1967. Adapted from the acting text made by Robert Kemp for Tyrone Guthrie's production for the Edinburgh Festival of 1948.

J. Small and F. Hall. *Sir David Lindsay's Works.* New York: Greenwood, 1969. This is a reprinting of the EETS Original Series xi, xix, xxxv, and xxxvii.

Dramatis Personae

Diligence, herald	Merchant
Rex Humanitas	Soutar, cobbler
Wantonness ⎫	Tailor
Placebo ⎬ courtiers	Jennie, Tailor's daughter
Solace ⎭	Soutar's wife
Lady Sensuality	Oppression
Hamliness	Abasse
Danger	Tailor's wife
Fund-Jonet, a bawd	Varlet
Good Counsel	Divine Correction

Flattery ⎫	Pauper
Falset ⎬ vices	Wilkin, Pardoner's boy
Deceit ⎭	John the Commonweal
Verity, True Religion	First Sergeant
Spirituality	Second Sergeant
Abbot	Covetise
Chastity	Scribe
Prioress	Theft
Parson	Pardoner (Flattery)
Temporality	Doctor

Length of the play: 4,629 lines.

Plot Summary

Diligence speaks the Prologue, which describes the action of the play to follow. Although Rex Humanitas (King Humanity) now avoids Correction, Truth, and Discretion, and lives with Lady Sensuality, he will through the aid of Divine Correction effect a complete reformation. The causes of his departure from virtue are the false courtiers Placebo, Solace, and Wantonness, who, along with the bawd Fund-Jonet and Flattery, Falset (False Report), and Deceit, point out effectively the domination of Lady Sensuality. Flattery disguises himself as a friar, explaining that friars have the most fun and are admitted everywhere. All three vice-fools change their names in a mock baptism — Deceit to Discretion, Flattery to Devotion, and Falset to Sapience — and ingratiate themselves with the King so that they become his treasurer, counsellor and confessor, and secretary. Good Counsel tries to approach the King, but is hurled out of the presence by the three false courtiers. Lady Verity (True Religion) is falsely accused of heresy and put in the stocks (along with Chastity) when she can find no home either with the spiritual or the temporal estates. At the entrance of Divine Correction, the vices flee — Deceit to the merchants, Falset to the crafts-men, and Flattery to the Spirituality. Sensuality is driven

back to Rome; Chastity, Good Counsel, and Truth are received by the King. Correction commands the latter to con-
vene a Parliament of the Three Estates to reform the country.
Placebo, Wantonness, and Solace are pardoned when they
plead ignorance of their evil and cite the example of the
clergy. Part I of the play ends with a salutary admonition by
Good Counsel to the young King.

Part II opens with the complaints of the Pauper, whose
cows have all been taken away by the clergy. A Pardoner
(Flattery in Disguise) tries to sell him remission of his sins,
but the Pauper is naturally more interested in obtaining
justice. Diligence announces the coming of the Three Estates,
who enter walking backwards as an indication of their persistence in vice. The King proposes methods of reform which
disturb Spirituality. John the Commonweal enters, exposes
and arrests the vices, and meets out charges of injustice all
around. Much stress is laid on the duty of clergymen to
preach and on abuses in the hierarchy. Means of correcting
the evils in the realm and the Church are thoroughly ex-
plored. Wrong-doers are questioned and rebuked, and a
Doctor preaches a model sermon. When the Bishop, Abbot,
Parson, and Prioress depart, John the Commonweal is solemnly instated in Parliament. The reforms are read; the Vices
are punished (except for Flattery, who helps hang his fel-
lows). The tone of the play is made clear in its ending. Folly
enters after the serious speeches of reformation, seeks the
King's justice against a sow, and preaches a mock sermon or
"sermon joyeux." The virtue Diligence ends the action of the
play on a note of gaiety:

> Let sum go drink, and som go dance:
> Menstrell, blaw vp ane brawell of France;
> Let se quha hobbils best.
> For I will run, incontinent,
> To the tavern, or ever I stent,
> And pray to God omnipotent,
> To send you all gude rest!

129

Comments

The *Satire of the Three Estates* is a Protestant "estates" play. The humor and comic elements of the play should not be obscured by its religious propaganda. The *Satire of the Three Estates* exposes folly not villainy. It is one of the few morality plays that can boast of a major, public, modern performance; it was acted in 1948 at the Edinburgh Festival.

Other "estates" plays:

> *Cobbler's Prophesy* (No. VII).
> *King John* (No. XXII).
> *Looking Glass for London and England* (No. XXVII).
> *Play of the Weather* (No. LVI).
> *Three Ladies of London* (No. XLVIII).
> *Three Lords and Three Ladies of London* (No. L).
> *Tide Tarrieth No Man* (No. LI).

See Coming of Death (Appendix I).

Critical Studies

Houk, Raymond. "Versions of Lindsay's *Satire of the Three Estates.*" *PMLA*, 55:396-405 (1940).

MacLaine, Allan H. *"Christis Kirk on the Grene* and Sir David Lindsay's *Satyre of the Thrie Estaits.*" *JEGP*, 56:596-601 (1957).

MacQueen, John. *"Ane Satyre of the Thre Estaites.*" *SSL*, 3:129-143 (1966).

Mill, Anna. "The Influence of Continental Drama on Lyndsay's *Satyre of the Thrie Estaitis.*" *MLR*, 25:425-442 (1930).

_____ *Medieval Plays in Scotland.* London: W. Blackwood and Sons, 1927. (Reprinted, New York: B. Blom, 1969).

_____ "The Original Version of Lindsay's *Satyre of the Thrie Estaitis.*" *SSL*, 6:67-75 (1969).

_____ "Representations of Lyndsay's *Satyre of the* Thrie Estaitis." *PMLA*, 47:636-651 (1932).

_____ "Representations of Lyndsay's *Satyre of the Thrie Estaitis.*" *PMLA*, 48:315-316 (1933).

Miller, Edwin. "The Christening in *The Three Estates.*" *MLN,* 60:42-44 (1945).

Tobin, Terence. "The Beginnings of Drama in Scotland." *ThS,* 8:1-16 (1967).

XLVI. SOMEBODY AND OTHERS or THE SPOILING OF LADY VERITY, c. 1550
(Anonymous)

Two leaves survive. No known title, printer, or date of publication.

Editions
S. R. Maitland. *List of Early Printed Books at Lambeth.* London, 1843.

*W. W. Greg. *Malone Society Collections,* II, 3 (1931).

Dramatis Personae
Somebody
Avarice
Minister
Verity
Simony

Length of the fragment: 140 lines.

Plot Summary
The speaker of the first line (probably Minister) curses Somebody. After the introduction of Avarice, Minister, who stands for false doctrine, states that Verity opposes him in all

131

things. Avarice offers Simony (disguised as Verity) as a new mistress for Minister, who says he can control the people but that he has no influence on Somebody. Minister, Simony, and Avarice plot the abduction of Verity. Verity asserts that she herself prophesied her own temporary deposition but looks forward to better days. The fragment ends here but the ending of the play can possibly be constructed from the French morality *La Verité Cachée,* of which it is an adaptation. Verité is freed from hiding by Aucun (Somebody), who also deposes Simonie. See Louis Petit de Julleville, *Répertoire* (Paris, 1886) pp. 101-102.

Comments

Although apparently a political play, it is difficult to determine the auspices under which *Somebody and Others* was written. A. Brandl sees Somebody to stand for Queen Mary (*Quellen des weltlichen Dramas,* p. lix). W. W. Greg sees the play as Protestant and suggests that Somebody be either Edward or Elizabeth — two rulers who re-asserted Protestantism after the Catholic resurgences following the deaths of Henry VIII and Mary I. (*Malone Society Collections* II, 3, p. 251-52).

XLVII. TEMPERANCE AND HUMILITY, c. 1530
(Anonymous)

One leaf survives, marked with the signature Aiij. According to Greg this signature occurs only in plays from the presses of de Worde, Pynson, and Skot.

Edition
W. W. Greg. *Malone Society Collections,* I,3 (1910).

Dramatis Personae
  Disobedience
  Temperance
  Humility

Length of the fragment: 62 lines.

Plot Summary
  Questioned by Disobedience, who is all-powerful through-out the land, Temperance and Humility introduce themselves. They deplore the control over most people that Disobedience enjoys and ask God to "banyshe this vyce from this countre/ And restore obedyence to euery place." Disobedience says that this restoration will never occur; furthermore, he will bring on many more of his confederates, among whom are his brother Adversity (alias Prosperity) and Audacity. The fragment ends here.

Comments
  From this one leaf A. Brandl suggests that the play is Catholic and comes from the reign of Mary I. If this is so, *Temperance and Humility* is closely akin to *Respublica* (No. XLIV). W. W. Greg points out, however, that typographical evidence suggests that the fragment was printed long before Mary's time.

Critical Studies
Craik, T. W. "The Political Interpretation of Two Tudor
    Interludes: *Temperance and Humility* and *Wealth and
    Health." RES*, n.s. 4:98-108 (1953).

XLVIII. THREE LADIES OF LONDON, 1581
(Robert Wilson?)

A right excellent and famous Comoedy called the three Ladies of London. Wherein is notablie declared and set forth, how by the means of Lucar, Loue and Conscience is so corrupted, that the one is married to Dissimulation, the other fraught with all abhomination. A perfect patterne for all Estates to looke into, and a worke right worthie to be marked. Written by R. W. as it hath been publiquely played. Roger Warde, 1584.

Editions
J. P. Collier. *Five Old Plays.* Roxburghe Club. London, 1851.
*Dodsley, VI.

Dramatis Personae
    Prologue
    Fame
    Love ⎫
    Conscience ⎬   three Ladies of London
    Lucre ⎭
    Simplicity
    Fraud ⎫
    Simony ⎬
    Usury ⎬   four vices
    Dissimulation ⎭
    Mercatore
    Artifex
    Lawyer
    Sincerity
    Hospitality
    Sir Nicholas Nemo
    Peter Pleaseman, a parson
    Gerontus, a Jew
    Cogging, Dissimulation's man

Tom Beggar
Willy Will
Judge of Turkey
Serviceable Diligence, the Constable
Officer
Judge Nemo
Clerk
Crier

Length of the play: approximately 1,800 lines.

Plot Summary

Love and Conscience lament that all men follow Lucre; Fame counsels patience and promises them a triple crown if they resist corruption. Simplicity joins with Dissimulation, Fraud, Simony, and Usury in seeking employment in London from any of the three Ladies dwelling there — Love, Conscience, and Lucre. Simplicity becomes Love's servant, but the four vices are sent packing to Lucre, who welcomes them joyfully.

Four suitors apply through the vices to obtain the favor of Lady Lucre. First, an Italian Mercatore promises to supply frivolous adornments for Englishmen in return for protection. Second, a poor craftsman (Artifex) begs Fraud to intercede with Lady Lucre for help because he finds it impossible to earn a living following the dictates of Conscience. Third, a lawyer, dissatisfied with the small wages received in pleading for Love and Conscience, offers his talents to the more desirable third Lady. The priest Sincerity soon learns that Love and Conscience have not the power to grant him a living and that he must make his request to Lady Lucre. Having no money to offer Simony (who has charge of these affairs), Sincerity must content himself with the parish of St. Nihil (Nothing) and the patronage of Sir Nicholas Nemo (no one).

The corruptive power of money becomes so advanced in London that Conscience and Love are turned out of their house by Usury. In contrast to the priest Sincerity, the worldly parson Peter Pleaseman easily obtains preferment from Simony once he has promised the latter one-half his first year's income. Usury murders Hospitality; Conscience is forced to seek her living selling brooms. Lucre announces the wedding of Dissimulation and Love, and succeeds even in corrupting Conscience, whose face is symbolically dabbed with ink from the "box of all abhomination." Dissimulation reviews the names of the wedding guests with his servant Cogging, and learns of a battle between Usury and Good Neighborhood and Liberality. The Jew Gerontus brings before the Judge of Turkey Mercatore, who has refused to repay borrowed money. The Mercatore is quite willing to become a Turk to be free from his debt; but the Jew refuses to be responsible for a man's denial of faith, and remits the entire debt. Simplicity is whipped for having consorted with thieves. Lucre, Conscience, and deformed Love stand trial and are condemned. Lucre is taken to hell along with Love. Conscience admits to her guilt and is sent to prison to await the general session.

Comments
   Three Ladies of London is a social "estates" morality and a companion piece to *The Three Lords and Three Ladies of London* (No. L).
   Other "estates" plays:
      Cobbler's Prophesy (No. VII).
      King John (No. XXII).
      Looking Glass for London and England (No. XXVII).
      Play of the Weather (No. LVI).
      Satire of the Three Estates (No. XLV).
      Three Lords and Three Ladies of London (No. L).
      Tide Tarrieth No Man (No. LI).

Critical Studies
Gatch, K. H. "Robert Wilson, Actor and Dramatist." Yale

University Dissertation, 1928.
Mann, Irene Rose. "A Lost Version of *The Three Ladies of London.*" *PMLA,* 59:586-589 (1944).
_____ "The Text of the Plays of Robert Wilson." University of Virginia Dissertation, 1942.

XLIX. THREE LAWS, 1530-36
(John Bale)

A Comedy concernynge thre lawes, of nature, Moses, & Christ, corrupted by the Sodomytes, Pharysees and Papystes. Compyled by Iohan Bale. Anno M. D. XXXVIII and lately imprented per Nicolaum Bamburgensem. Basle, 1558.

Editions
A. Schroeer. *Anglia,* V (1882).
*Farmer, 1907 (*Dramatic Writings of John Bale*).

Dramatis Personae
Into five personages may the parts of this Comedy be divided:

The Prolocutor ⎫
Christian Faith ⎬ the first
Infidelity ⎭

The Law of Moses ⎫
Idolatry ⎬ the second
Hypocrisy ⎭

The Law of Nature ⎫
Covetousness ⎬ the third
False Doctrine ⎭

The Law of Christ ⎫
Ambition   ⎬   the fourth
Sodomy   ⎭

Deus Pater ⎫
Vindicta Dei ⎭   the fifth

Length of the play: 2,081 lines.

Plot Summary

God the Father instructs the Three Laws in their duties toward man: first, instruction and maintenance of man's innocence by the Law of Nature; second, correction after the fall by the Law of Moses; third, salvation by the Law of Christ. The next three acts witness the corruption of the Three Laws by six vices sent, two at a time, by the chief Vice, Infidelity. All are the special representatives of the Catholic Church and of the anti-Christ Pope, "the master of Gomor and of Sodom." Idolatry and Sodomy corrupt Law of Nature; Avarice and Ambition, by means of "Sophistry, Philosophy, and Logic," subvert the Law of Moses; False Doctrine and Hypocrisy defile the Law of Christ. In Act V, entitled the Restoration of Divine Law, Vindicta Dei (God's Vengeance) confronts and punishes the Vice Infidelity with water, the sword, and fire, instruments which are symbolic of the Vice's corruption of the Three Laws. The Three Laws of Nature, Moses, and Christ are restored to their former states. Christian Faith, the representative of the true Church of Christ (Protestantism), is welcomed and instated by God the Father.

Comments

In spite of the Protestant auspices of *Three Laws,* there is much of the medieval in the play: configuration of three, the debate, the use of Latin and not English for Scripture. *Three Laws* is replete with interesting allusions to real people — mostly slanderous attempts to defame the Catholic Church and especially the Pope. The allusion closest to 16th century England is that which warns the audience against subscribing to any of the ideas of Reginald Pole. The speech of Sodomy may well be the first treatment of homosexuality on the English stage.

Other Protestant plays:
Conflict of Conscience (No. IX).
King Darius (No. XXI).
King John (No. XXII).
New Custom (No. XL).

Critical Studies
Blatt, Thora B. *The Plays of John Bale: A Study of Ideas, Technique and Style.* Copenhagen: G. E. C. Gad, 1968.
Davies, W. T. "A Bibliography of Bale." In *Oxford Bibliographical Society, Proceedings and Papers,* 5:203-279 (1936-39).

L. THREE LORDS AND THREE LADIES OF LONDON, 1589
(Robert Wilson)

The pleasant and Stately Morall of the three Lordes and three Ladies of London. With the great Ioy and Pompe, Solemnized at their Mariages: Commically interlaced with much honest Mirth, for pleasure and recreation, among many Morall obseruations and other important matters of due Regard. by R. W. R. Jones, 1590.

Editions
J. P. Collier. *Five Old Plays.* Roxburghe Club. London, 1851.
*Dodsley, VI.

L

Dramatis Personae

Policy
Pomp — Three Lords of London
Pleasure
Nemo, a grave old man
Love
Lucre — Three Ladies of London
Conscience
Honest Industry
Pure Zeal — Three Sages
Sincerity
Pride
Ambition — Three Lords of Spain
Tyranny
Desire
Delight — Three Lords of Lincoln
Devotion
Simplicity, a poor Freeman of London
Painful Penury, his wife
Fealty
Shealty — Two Heralds-at-Arms
Falsehood
Double-Dealing — Servants of Fraud and Dissimulation
Wit
Wealth — Pages to the Three Lords of London
Will
Shame
Treachery — Pages to the Three Lords of Spain
Terror
Sorrow, a Jailer
Diligence, an officer
Fraud
Usury
Dissimulation — Four Gallants
Simony

Length of the play: approximately 2,300 lines.

Plot Summary

The Three Lords Policy, Pomp, and Pleasure resolve to wed the Three Ladies of London, Conscience, Love, and Lucre. A predictable difficulty arises when all three Lords declare for Lady Lucre, but they defer the resoltuon of the problem until they have freed all three Ladies from the hands of Nemo, who has kept them prisoner after their scandalous marriages to three Spaniards. Will, Wit, and Wealth discuss their masters' shields and mottos, and converse with the ballad-monger Simplicity and his wife Painful Penury. Nemo agrees to release the Ladies from prison provided that he may bestow them on the Lords as he secs fit.

The four vices Dissimulation, Fraud, Simony, and Usury meet in anticipation of the release from prison of their former mistress Lady Lucre. They tell of their adventures since their banishment, but are interrupted when Sorrow enters with the three Ladies. Sitting on stones marked Remorse (Conscience), Charity (Love), and Care (Lucre), the three grief-stricken Ladies receive their former servants. Lucre informs the four vices that since her imprisonment she can no longer employ them as she used to do. While the Three Ladies are being displayed before the Three Lords, Falsehood and Double-Dealing bring new clothes for Lucre and Love. Nemo exposes them as servants of Fraud and Dissimulation and, in their place, calls in Honest Industry, Pure Zeal, and Sincerity to dress Lucre, Love, and Conscience.

Painful Penury and Simplicity are cheated by Fraud posing as a foreign craftsman. On the day appointed for the bestowal of the Three Ladies on the Three Lords, Nemo discovers that the three men all desire Lucre. Introducing Conscience as Lucre, he causes Pleasure to desire her and then reveals the ruse. Diligence interrupts with a message that the Spanish are preparing an armada to attack London. As the Three Lords prepare themselves for the attack, they promise to return to the Ladies once the victory is assured. Because the imminent war with the Spanish has caused Londoners to return to piety, the gallants Fraud, Dissimulation, and Simony decide to join the Spanish side until the outcome one way or the other is certain. Usury, however, thinks it best to remain in London.

The Spanish Lords Pride, Ambition, and Tyranny with their pages Shame, Treachery, and Terror enter with great show and stand opposite the Three Lords. The two heralds Fealty and Shealty each explain in detail the symbolism of their masters' shields and mottos. When a physical confrontation almost occurs, the Spanish prove their cowardice by running. Disguised and using aliases, Fraud (Skill) and Dissimulation (Fair Semblance) appeal to Policy and Pleasure for work. Undisguised, Usury tenders a like appeal to Pomp, but is rejected and branded. Fraud is sent to Newgate, but Dissimulation escapes and later returns to help his friends. Desire, Delight, and Devotion, the Three Lords of Lincoln, also desire to wed the Three Ladies. With a bit of clever casuistry on the part of the London Lords, the three Country Lords become the husbands not of the Three Ladies but of the stones Care, Charity, and Remorse on which the Ladies used to sit. The play ends in the wedding of Policy to Love, Pleasure to Conscience, and Pomp to Lucre.

Comments

The Three Lords and the Three Ladies of London is a continuation of the *Three Ladies of London* (No. XLVIII) and, like it, a social "estates" morality. *The Three Lords,* more than its earlier companion, is filled with gallantry, courtly love, and much ritual pageantry.

Other "estates" plays:

Cobbler's Prophesy (No. VII).
King John (No. XXII).
Looking Glass for London and England (No. XXVII).
Play of the Weather (No. LVI).

Satire of the Three Estates (No. XLV).
Three Ladies of London (No. XLVIII).
Tide Tarrieth No Man (No. LI).

Critical Studies

Gatch, K. H. "Robert Wilson, Actor and Dramatist." Yale University Disserations, 1928.

Mann, Irene Rose. "The Text of the Plays of Robert Wilson." University of Virginia Dissertation, 1942.

Mithal, H. S. D. "'Chipping Norton a Mile from Chapel of the Heath'." *N&Q,* 6:193 (1959).

_____ "The Variants in Robert Wilson's *The Three Lords of London.*" *The Library,* Ser. 5, 18:142-144 (1963).

Nathanson, Leonard. "Variants in Robert Wilson's *The Three Lords.*" *The Library,* Ser. 5, 13:57-59 (1958).

LI. TIDE TARRIETH NO MAN, 1576
(George Wapull)

The Tyde tarryeth no Man. A Moste Pleasant and merry Commody, right pythie and full of delight. Compiled by George Wapull. Hugh Jackson, 1576.

Editions

J. P. Collier. *Illustrations of Early English Popular Literature,* II. London, 1864.

*Ruhl. *Jarhbuch,* XLIII (1907).

Dramatis Personae

Four persons may easily play it.

1. The Prologue, Hurtful Help, the Tenant, Faithful Few, for one.

2. Painted Profit, No Good Neighborhood, the Courtier (Willing-to-Win-Worship), Wastefulness, Christianity, Correction, for another.
3. Courage the Vice, Debtor, for another.
4. Feigned Furtherance, Greediness the Merchant, Wantonness the Woman, the Servant, Authority, and Despair, for another.

Length of the play: 1,879 lines.

Plot Summary

The idea expressed in the title receives dual treatment. The evil forces opt for immediate abandonment to pleasure because there may be no tomorrow, and the virtuous figures advise good living for the same reason. The Vice Courage and his friends Hurtful Help, Painted Profit, and Feigned Furtherance state their philosophy of employing time and also their common purpose of leading men to hell. The first two victims are the land-owner Greediness and No Good Neighborhood, who covets a piece of land owned by Greediness. Promising help to both but solicitous only for their downfall, the vices enlist the aid of Feigned Furtherance to expedite the business of property transfer. The Courtier Willing-to-Win-Worship next comes under the vices' influence. Possessed of little money, he is about to return to the country when Hurtful Help and Feigned Furtherance are sent by Courage to help in obtaining a loan from Greediness. A victimized Tenant wanders on stage looking for "constant and just" Christianity — a reminder that the forces of good are exiled but not dead. Courage arranges the marriage of Wantonness, a young girl of fourteen overanxious to marry, to Wastefulness, a young man, who then is forced to satisfy his new wife's craving for luxury. The bitter end of all waywardness next receives dramatic treatment as a miserable Debtor (possibly the Courtier) is apprehended and carried off by the Sergeant. Christianity and Faithful Few attempt in vain to reason with

Greediness. Wastefulness, now a beggar, is also driven by Despair to insanity, dies and is condemned to hell. The forces of good prevail, and Courage is carried to jail by Correction.

Comments

The *Tide Tarrieth No Man* is a social "estates" morality. The central Mankind figure is here bifurcated into Christianity and Faithful Few, who are prone to good, and the evil companions (representatives of the classes of society), who are prone to evil. To the modern reader a Vice named Courage may seem a contradiction in terms. Courage should be taken in its medieval sense of an irrational use of energy and will (B. Spivack, *Shakespeare and the Allegory of Evil,* p. 232).

Other "estates" plays:

Cobbler's Prophesy (No. VII).

King John (No. XXII).

Looking Glass for London and England (No. XXVII).

Play of the Weather (No. LVI).

Satire of the Three Estates (No. XLV).

Three Ladies of London (No. XLVIII).

Three Lords and Three Ladies of London (No. L).

Other plays with a bifurcated Mankind figure:

Enough is as Good as a Feast (No. XI).

Glass of Government (No. XIII).

Like Will to Like (No. XXV).

Nice Wanton (No. XLI).

Trial of Treasure (No. LIII).

See Coming of Death (Appendix I).

LII. TOM TYLER AND HIS WIFE, 1550-80
(Anonymous)

Tom Tylere and His Wife. A passing merrie Interlude. 1598. No known printer. Reprinted as *Tom Tyler and His Wife. An Excellent Old Play, As it was Printed and Acted about a hundred Years ago.* The Second Impression. 1661. No known printer.

Editions
F. E. Schelling. *PMLA,* 15:253-89 (1900).
*Farmer, 1906.
G. C. Moore Smith and W. W. Greg. *MSR,* 1910.

Dramatis Personae
Destiny, a sage person
Desire, the Vice
Tom Tyler, a laboring man
Strife, Tom Tyler's wife
Sturdy, a gossip
Tipple, an ale-wife
Tom Tayler, an artificer
Patience, a sage person

Length of the play: 927 lines.

Plot Summary
Desire seeks out Destiny with a problem. It happened that Tom Tyler, wishing a wife, sought Desire to help him. Desire obliged, but Tom had the misfortune to marry a shrew for which he blames both Desire and Destiny. They assert that they did only what they were bidden to do, and that the outcome is not their fault but Tom's. They leave to avoid Tom, who enters singing about his cruel wife named Strife. To escape her beatings, he has decided to devote himself to his work and goes inside. Strife appears boasting of her absolute

146

control over the mouselike Tom, and is followed on stage by
the gossip Sturdy and the ale-wife Tipple. Strife maliciously
tells the other two women that she wishes Tom were there so
that she could demonstrate her great power to them by
beating him. When he does enter to fetch a pot of beer, Strife
accuses him of cheating his employers by leaving his work
and beats him back to his job. Exulting in feminine victory,
the three women rejoice in singing and dancing. When they
go in, Tom returns declaring that he would be a very happy
man indeed if only he were free of his terrible wife. His problem is made known to Tom Tayler, who offers to help.
Tayler's plan is to change clothes with Tom Tyler and to give
Strife the beating she deserves. Tom Tyler leaves the stage
while his friend beats the unknowing Strife into submission.
She goes to bed ill. Tayler sends Tom in to her, but only after
they have celebrated by singing "The Tying of the Mare."
When Strife is once again alone, Sturdy and Tipple listen to
the wailing of the bruised wife. Evidently tiring of Strife's
lamenting and eager to tell others of what has passed, Sturdy
and Tipple decide to go to town. Tom, finding Strife lying
down ill, politely blames his now submissive wife for what
has happened to her. He then makes his worst mistake – he
tells Strife that it was not he at all who gave the beating but
Tom Tayler in his clothes. Strife naturally rises up in a rage,
resumes her former control and commences to beat the weak
and foolish Tom. Sturdy and Tipple advise Tom to leave if he
values his life. Strife declares herself in good health again and
invites the other two women to join in the song "Tom Tyler
was a Trifler." Destiny, Tom Tyler, and Tom Tayler conclude
that poor Tom was born to be beaten and that he should
make the best of his marriage. Strife joins them with her
customary verbal abuse. She is interrupted by Patience, who
gives salutary advice to all concerned, accepts their apologies,
and leads them in two final songs and a dance.

Comments

    Tom Tyler, a hybrid play, is clearly farcical and contains much realistic detail, but its didacticism and personified abstractions link it to the more serious homiletic drama. Although all plays of this period contained some singing and dancing, *Tom Tyler* is replete with the popular songs of its day. "John Come Kiss Me" is mentioned but not sung. Others that are sung are "The Tying of the Mare;" "Tom Tyler was a Trifler;" "Patience Entreateth Good Fellows All;" and "Though Pinching Be a Privy Pain."

LIII. TRIAL OF TREASURE, 1567
(Anonymous)

A new and mery Enterlude, called the Trial of Treasure, newly set forth, and neuer before this tyme imprinted. Thomas Purfoot, 1567.

Editions
J. O. Halliwell. Percy Society, XXVIII (1850).
Dodsley, III.
*Farmer, 1906.

Dramatis Personae
    First: Sturdiness, Contentation, Visitation, Time.
    Second: Lust, Sapience, Consolation.
    Third: Preface, Just, Pleasure, Greedy-Gut.
    Fourth: Elation, Trust (a woman), Treasure (a woman).
    Fifth: Inclination (the Vice).

Length of the play: 1,148 lines.

Plot Summary

Affirming the temporality of all things terrestrial, the Preface announces the play's title and trusts that the godly will not take offense. The two Mankind figures Lust and Just meet each other in an initial confrontation which culminates in a wrestling match. Their incompatibility being thus verified, Lust and Just separate to follow each his own road — one to damnation, the other to salvation. The Vice Inclination advises Lust and his new companion Sturdiness to become disciples of Epicurus, and offers them the assistance of Elation and Greedy-Gut. As Sturdiness remains behind to ward off Just, Inclination proposes to lead Lust and a new companion Carnal Cogitation to a place of pleasure. After a conversation on the subject of heavenly versus worldly treasure, Sapience and Just meet with Inclination, and engage in a fight in which the latter is tightly bound and left helpless. Having released Inclination, Lust tells him of his desire for Lady Treasure. Thoroughly pleased with Lust's choice of the "great goddess," Inclination, Greedy-Gut, and Elation lead Lust to a rendez-vous with Lady Treasure at the house of Carnal Cogitation. Just, Trust, and Contention cite examples from antiquity confirming the transience of worldly goods and depart singing a hymn. Inclination, Lust and his new mistress Lady Treasure are joined by Treasure's brother Pleasure. Lust is delighted with his good fortune, but the asides of Inclination warn of impending ruin. God's Visitation claims Pleasure as a proper reward for virtuous Just and leaves Lust in pain with the new useless Lady Pleasure as companion. Treasure promises to bring about the return of Pleasure, but Time intervenes to bring an end to their revelry. Lust and Treasure are turned to dust and rust and Just prospers with Consolation. Just once again shackles Inclination, who nevertheless vows continual rebellion against those who would be good. Time reiterates the moral of the play, and Consolation bids farewell to the audience.

Comments

Significant is the bifurcation of the central Mankind figure into Just and Lust. This is the only extant English morality in which appears the character Time.

Other plays with a bifurcated Mankind figure:

Enough is as Good as a Feast (No. XI).
Glass of Government (No. XIII).
Like Will to Like (No. XXV).
Nice Wanton (No. XLI).
Tide Tarrieth No Man (No. LI).

See Coming of Death (Appendix I).
Psychomachia (Appendix V).

Critical Studies

Daw, E. B. "Two Notes on *The Trial of Treasure.*" *MP*, 15:53-55 (1917).

Greg, W. W. *"The Trial of Treasure, 1567.* A Study in Ghost." *The Library*, Ser. 3, 1:28-35 (1910).

Oliver, Leslie. "William Wager and *The Trial of Treasure.*" *HLQ*, 9:419-429 (1946).

LIV. VIRTUOUS AND GODLY SUSANNA, 1568-69
(Thomas Garter)

The Commody of the moste vertuous and Godlye Susanna, neuer before this tyme Printed. Compiled by Thomas Garter. Hugh Jackson, 1578.

Edition

B. I. Evans and W. W. Greg. *MSR*, 1937.

Dramatis Personae
Eight persons may easily play it.
1. The Prologue and the Gaoler for one
2. Joachim and Judex (Judge) for another
3. Satan and Voluptas another
4. Sensualitas alone
5. Susanna alone
6. Helchia, True Report, Ancilla (girl servant), another
7. Ill Report the Vice, and Crier another
8. Helchia's wife, Daniel, Servus, Serva for another
(Sensualitas and Voluptas also go by the names Elders or
Judges. In the play the gaoler is always referred to as
Bailey. The Vice Ill Report need not change his dress or
clothes to play the Crier. See Evans and Greg, *MSR,*
Introduction, p. vi).

Length of the play: 1,450 lines.

Plot Summary
Vexed that the woman Susanna in Babylon has resisted all
his tricks and temptations, the Devil calls upon his son Ill
Report to cause her downfall in any way he can devise. Ill
Report meets Voluptas and Sensuality (the two Elders or
Judges), and, for a fee of £10, promises to help them satisfy
themselves with Susanna. The righteous Joachim and his
beautiful wife Susanna meet with the two Elders, who, upon
seeing Susanna, become more desirous of her than ever.
(Except for the activities of the Vice, Ill Report, and several
incursions into Sixteenth Century English court life, the plot
follows that of Scripture.) The two Elders hide in the or-
chard, break in upon Susanna, and are rejected outright. The
trial follows, Daniel is called in to assist, Susanna is vindi-
cated, and the evil Elders are exposed and executed. True
Report and the goaler next seek out Ill Report, who is hanged
and received back into hell by the Devil. Joachim, Susanna,
and their friends Helchia and his wife rejoice and thank God.

151

Comments

Virtuous and Godly Susanna is a hybrid "virtue" play.
Other "virtue" plays:

Appius and Virginia (No. III).
Godly Queen Hester (No. XIV).
Life and Repentance of Mary Magdalene (No. XXIV).
Patient and Meek Grissill (No. XLII).

Critical Studies

Blackburn, Ruth Harriett. "Tudor Biblical Drama." *DA,*
17:1746-1747 (1951).

Evans, B. "The Lost *Commody of Susanna." TLS,* May 2,
1936, p. 372.

Herrick, Marvin T. "Susanna and the Elders in Sixteenth
Century Drama." In *Studies in Honor of T. W. Baldwin.*
Ed. Don Cameron Allen. Urbana, Ill.: University of Illinois
Press, 1958, pp. 125-135.

Pilger, Robert. "Die dramatisierungen der Susanna im 16.
Jahrhundert." *ZDP,* 11:129-217 (1889).

Roston, Murray. *Biblical Drama in England from the Middle
Ages to the Present Day.* London: Faber and Faber, 1968.

LV. WEALTH AND HEALTH, 1553-57
(Anonymous)

*An enterlude of Welth, and Helth, full of sport and mery
Pastyme, newly at this tyme Imprinted.* No known printer or
date of publication; the play was entered on the books of the
Stationers' Company for 1557-58.

Editions
W. W. Greg and P. Simpson. *MSR,* 1907.
*Farmer, 1907.
F. Holthausen. Festschrift des Universität Kiel. 1908 (rev.
ed. 1922).

Dramatis Personae
Four may easily play this play.
Wealth	Ill-Will	Hance
Health	Shrewd Wit	Remedy
Liberty		

Length of the play: 964 lines.

Plot Summary
Wealth and Health at first dispute which of them is the
more important, but Liberty's claim for his own indispens-
ability proliferates the disagreement so that Ill-Will, the Vice,
joins the contentious group. At the departure of Wealth,
Health, and Liberty, Ill-Will joins with the cutpurse Shrewd
Wit. Hance, a drunken Fleming of almost unintelligible
speech, interrupts their plot to destroy the tenuous unity of
the virtues, and, quite surprisingly, manages to get off without being made the object of a prank. Ill-Will and Shrewd
Wit, under the names of Will and Wit, enter the service of the
virtues. Having met with the powerful and noble Good
Remedy, but unaware of their need for him, the virtues thank
him for his solicitude and promise to call if need should arise.
Ill-Will and Shrewd Wit easily succeed in disturbing the harmony of the virtues and are found out by Good Remedy,
who, with Health now ailing from the recent troubles, confronts the two vices and sends them to jail. Harmony is
restored, Elizabeth is praised and the Commonality upheld.

Comments
Wealth and Health is a social morality. The playwright uses

Hance to satire immigrant Flemish workers. He is one of the first characters on the English stage to speak in broken English.

Other "social" plays:
>
> *Albion Knight* (No. I).
> *All for Money* (No. II).
> *Impatient Poverty* (No. XVIII).
> *Liberality and Prodigality* (No. XXIII).
> *Like Will to Like* (No. XXV).

See *Cobbler's Prophesy* (No. VII) for a list of the "estates" plays, all of which are "social" pieces.

Critical Studies

Bang-Kaupt, Willy. "Note on 11. 388-428 and 750-758 (of *Wealth and Health*)." *Malone Society Collections,* I, pp. 7-14.

Craik, T. W. "The Political Interpretation of Two Tudor Interludes: *Temperance and Humility* and *Wealth and Health.*" *RES,* n.s. 4:98-108 (1953).

Hunter, Mark. "Notes on the Interlude of *Wealth and Health.*" *MLR,* 3:366-369 (1907).

Pineas, Rainer. "The Revision of *Wealth and Health.*" *PQ,* 44:560-562 (1965).

LVI. WEATHER, Play of the (1530-33)
(John Heywood)

The play of the wether. A new and a very mery enterlude of all maner wethers made by Iohn Heywood. William Rastell, 1533.

Editions
Brandl.
A. W. Pollard. *Representative English Comedies.* New York, 1903.
*J. S. Farmer. *Dramatic Writings of John Heywood.* 1905.
Adams.
M. Hussey and S. Agarwala. *The Play of the Weather by John Heywood and other Tudor Comedies Adapted into Modern English.* With Introduction. New York: Theatre Arts, 1968.

Dramatis Personae

Jupiter, a god	The Water-Miller
Merry-Report, the vice	The Wind-Miller
The Gentleman	The Gentlewoman
The Merchant	The Laundress
The Ranger	A Boy, the least (smallest) that can play

Length of the play: 1,254 lines.

Plot Summary

Dissatisfied with the irreconcilable and constant ill will between Saturn (cold), Phebus (heat), Eolus (wind), and Phebe (rain), Jupiter decrees that he will moderate a hearing to decide which type of weather is most desirable. The Vice Merry-Report easily ingratiates himself with the god and is sent on his way to collect various suitors, each to plead for his own preference in weather. Merry-Report first brings in a gentleman who desires weather suitable for hunting and other occupations necessary for the preservation of the nobility. A merchant bids for weather suitable for travelling, that is, not stormy but with moderate and changing wind. This, he argues, will enable merchants to import and export easily, thereby increasing the national wealth. Next, the Ranger opts for violent weather to stir things up in the forest, but Merry-

Report does not permit him to approach Jupiter. A long debate follows between the Water-Miller and the Wind-Miller, but they too are forbidden by Merry-Report to appear before Jupiter. The Gentlewoman desires only shady, calm weather so that her beauty will not be impaired. She is opposed by the Laundress, who needs sunshine to dry her clothes. The last suitor is a boy who wants continual snow with which to make snowballs. Feigning the lack of a solution to the problem of satisfying everyone, Merry-Report sums up the suits for Jupiter, who calls all the suitors together. The decree is that there will be all kinds of weather so that each person may in turn prosper in his own calling.

Comments

This "debate" play is included with the moralities because of the Vice Merry-Report and because it is an early example of the "estates" play.

Other "estates" plays:

Cobbler's Prophesy (No. VII).
King John (No. XXII).
Looking Glass for London and England (No. XXVII).
Satire of the Three Estates (No. XLV).
Three Ladies of London (No. XLVIII).
Three Lords and Three Ladies of London (No. L).
Tide Tarrieth No Man (No. LI).
See also *All for Money* (No. II).
Play of Love (No. XXVIII).

Critical Studies

Adams, Joseph Quincy. "Lucian A Source for Heywood's *Play of the Weather." MLN,* 22:262 (1907).

Bevington, David M. "Is John Heywood's *Play of the Weather* Really About the Weather?" *RenD,* 7:11-19 (1964).

Cameron, Kenneth W. *John Heywood's Play of the Wether, A Study in Early Tudor Drama.* Raleigh, N. C.: The Thistle Press, 1941.

Canzler, David George. "A Concordance to the Dramatic Works of John Heywood." *DA,* 21:3768-3769 (1961).
———— "Quarto Editions of *Play of the Wether.*" *PBSA,* 62:313-19 (1968).
Craik, T. W. "Experiment and Variety in John Heywood's Plays." *RenD,* 7:6-11 (1964).
Greg, W. W. "Notes on Some Early Plays. . . "The *Play of the Weather.*" *The Library,* Ser. 4, 9:44-56 (1930).
Hillebrand, H. N. "On the Authorship of the Interludes attributed to John Heywood." *MP,* 13:267-280 (1915).
Phy, Wesley. "The Chronology of John Heywood's Plays." *ES,* 14:27-41 (1940).

LVII. WISDOM WHO IS CHRIST or
MIND, WILL, AND UNDERSTANDING, 1461-85
(Anonymous)

Macro MS. now Folger V. a. 354. First printed in 1882 by the New Shakespeare Society and then in its complete form in 1904 by the EETS.

Editions

W. B. D. Turnbull. Abbotsford Club. Edinburgh, 1837.
F. J. Furnivall. *Digby Mysteries.* New Shakespeare Society, 1882. Reprinted in *EETS,* Extra Series, 1xx, 1896. [Only the first 754 lines of the play, as they survive in the Digby MS.]
*F. J. Furnivall and A. W. Pollard. *EETS,* Extra Series, xci, 1904.
Mark Eccles. *EETS,* No. 262, 1969.

Dramatis Personae
    Wisdom of Christ
    Anima (Soul)
    Anima's Five Wits as Five Virgins
    The Three Powers of every Christian soul:
        Mind
        Will
        Understanding
    Lucifer
    A shrewd Boy
    Mind's Six retainers: Indignation
                          Sturdiness
                          Malice
                          Hastiness
                          Revenge
                          Discord
        Maintenance
    Understanding's six false Jurors: Wrong
                                  Slight
                                  Doubleness
                                  Falsehood
                                  Ravine
                                  Deceit
        Perjury
    Will's six women: three disguised as Gallants, and three as
                  Matrons
    Minstrels: trumpeters, bagpipers, a hornpiper
    Six [seven are needed] small boys in the likeness of Devils.
    (Only Wisdom, Anima, Mind, Will, Understanding, and
    Lucifer speak. Maintenance and Perjury are not separate
    characters; Mind becomes Maintenance and Understanding
    becomes Perjury.)

Length of the play: 1,168 lines.

Plot Summary

The opening lines of instruction to Anima by Wisdom are pure homiletics dealing with such topics as man's dignity as the image of God, the excellence of wisdom and love, the necessity for man's obedience, the inheritance of Adam's sin, Christ's redemption of man, the sacraments, and the dual division of the soul into Sensuality and Reason. Dressed as five virgins, Anima's Five Wits enter in procession and are exhorted by Wisdom always to remain spiritually clean. We are then introduced to the three powers of the soul: MIND, WILL, and UNDERSTANDING. The instruction continues; we learn that Faith derives from Mind, Hope from Understanding, and Charity from Will, and that the enemies of the three powers of the soul are the World, the Flesh, and the Devil. After Anima has thanked God for his divine favor and goodness, a procession is formed, and they leave the stage in the following order: the Five Wits singing "Tota pulchra es" (a hymn to the Blessed Virgin), Anima, Wisdom, and last, Mind, Will, and Understanding.

Dressed as a devil but underneath as a gallant, Lucifer expounds on his reasons for hating mankind, and vents his anger in proud boasting of his future victory over his human prey. Next he assails Mind by posing the following case: should a man give up wife and family to devote himself to contemplation? His arguments against the monastic life are based on the examples of study, penance, and flattering preachers. He also postulates that the rigors of contemplative life lead to despair and madness, and opts instead for fine dress, riches, begetting children, and wine. Thus he converts Mind, Will, and Understanding, who vow to live as do the already notorious French. Their path downward is next mapped by Lucifer — from Pride to Covetousness, to Lechery, and, finally, to Despair. Mind, Will, and Understanding enter dressed in fine new robes symbolic of their worldly conversion. Will is attracted to women; Mind possesses elequence; noble relatives, and honor; Understanding glories in his riches.

After a song, we learn of their new occupations: Mind is in the employ of great personages whom he protects from the law; Understanding practices simony and perjury; Will spends more money than he has and enjoys a life of immorality. The result is that social mahem reigns because of personal decadence. Mind (who has become Maintenance) brings in his followers who are Indignation, Sturdiness, Malice, Hastiness, Vengeance, and Discord. Dressed with images of lions as crests, and, accompanied by trumpeters, they exhibit themselves in a dance. Similarly, Understanding (who has become Perjury) introduces Wrong, Slight, Doubleness, Falsehood, Ravine, and Deceit, all of whom are dressed as rich jurors. Will (now Lechery) summons Recklessness, Idleness, Surfeit, Greediness, Adultry, and Fornication, three of which are dressed as gallants and three as women. After a dance, Mind, Will, and Understanding banish the dancers and speak once more of their future at St. Paul's (Mind), Westminster (Understanding), and the stews (Will).

The Three Powers pursue their worldly careers until Wisdom enters to remind them of approaching Death. Heedless of the virtue, they even yet persist in their worldliness. Further to demonstrate their fall from grace, the now ugly and disfugured Anima enters "fouler than a fiend." Seven small boys dressed as devils and representing the Seven Deadly Sins dart from beneath Anima's mantle, pointing out dramatically in whose possession she is. Having seen the visible results of their sins, Mind, Will, and Understanding repent and leave the stage with Anima singing sadly "in the manner of Passion week." Wisdom next insists on true repentance and confession, and follows with an explanation of the nine points most pleasing to God which are a combination of the two great Commandments with the corporeal works of mercy. Anima, the Five Wits, and Mind, Will, and Understanding enter in their original dress to signify their return to grace. Anima and Wisdom (dressed as Christ) affirm their union and end the play with the desire that the audience avoid sin.

160

Comments

There is much opportunity in *Wisdom* for elaborate costumes and stately processions; the MS gives unusually complete directions for costumes and movments of actors. In fact, *Wisdom* has more merit as a pageant than it does as a play. Its structure is similar to that of *Hickscorner* (No. XVI). Although primarily an exhortation to virtue, *Wisdom* offers many comments on fifteenth century society.

Critical Studies

Bevington, David. "Political Satire in the Morality *Wisdom Who is Christ.*" *Renaissance Papers* (1963) pp. 41-51.

Fifield, Merle. *The Castle in the Circle.* Ball State Monograph 6. Muncie Ind.: Ball State University Press, 1967. [Staging of *Pride of Life* (No. XLIII), *Wisdom Who is Christ, Mankind* (No. XXXII), and *Everyman* (No. XII).]

_____ "The Use of Doubling and 'Extras' in *Wisdom Who is Christ.*" *BSUF,* 6:65-68 (1965).

Green, Joseph Coleman. "The Medieval Morality of *Wisdom Who is Christ.*" Vanderbilt University Dissertation, 1938.

Molloy, Rev. John J. *A Theological Interpretation for the Moral Play, Wisdom Who is Christ.* Washington, D. C.: Catholic University of America Press, 1952.

Schmidt, Karl. "Die Digbyspiele." *Anglia,* 8:371-404 (1885).

Smart, Walter Kay. *Some English and Latin Sources and Parallels for the Morality of Wisdom.* Menasha, Wisconsin: G. Banta, 1912.

Smith, Sister Frances. "Wisdom and the Personification of Wisdom in Middle English Literature before 1500." Catholic University of America Dissertation, 1935.

LVIII. WIT AND SCIENCE, 1536-46
(John Redford)

The first part of the play is missing, but it ends with the following colophon: *Thus endyeth the Play of Wyt and Science, made by Master Jhon* [sic] *Redford.*"

Editions
J. O. Halliwell. *Shakespeare Society Papers,* 1848.
*Manly, I.
Farmer, 1907.
A. Brown and W. W. Greg. *MSR,* 1951.

Dramatis Personae

Wit	Idleness
Science	Shame
Reason	Comfort
Experience	Quickness
Confidence	Strength
Honest Recreation	Fame
Study	Riches
Diligence	Favor
Instruction	Worship
Tediousness	

Length of the play: 1,051 lines.

Plot Summary
Similar in plot to the other Wit plays and employing the same chivalric metaphor, *Wit and Science* begins with the intentions of young Wit to marry Reason's daughter Science. Having received a gift of a "glass of Reason" from Reason, Wit offers Science a picture of himself and asks in turn for a token from her. Reason sees no obstacle to the union of Wit and Science provided that Wit prove himself worthy. Although he maintains Study and Diligence, Wit falls into the

hands of Tediousness when he refuses to follow Instruction. Honest Recreation, Comfort, Quickness, and Strength, all sent by Reason, find Wit unconscious on the ground and revive him with a song. In spite of the sobering admonitions of Reason, Wit next falls prey to Idleness, who paints Wit's face and dresses him in the clothes of Ignorance. Confidence brings the Sword of Comfort from Lady Science, but is unable to recognize Wit.

To the accompaniment of singing provided by Fame, Favor, Riches, and Worship, Lady Science and her mother Experience solemnly enter in preparation for a meeting with the intended bridegroom. The meeting takes place, but Wit is mistaken for Ignorance and rejected by Science. He discovers the Sword of Comfort is missing, and sees his own disfigurement when he looks into the mirror Reason had given him earlier. Repenting his delinquency, he allows himself to be whipped by Shame, and then receives Study, Diligence, and Instruction whom he had previously neglected. Confidence enters with the Sword of Comfort and presents Science with a golden heart from Wit. With the help of Study, Diligence, and Instruction, Wit climbs Mount Parnassus and slays Tediousness whose head is impaled on Wit's sword. Confidence reports that Lady Science witnessed the ordeal from an adjacent mountain and will now marry Wit. He receives a gown of knowledge, and, in the presence of Experience and Reason, weds Lady Science.

Comments

Wit and Science is an education or "youth" morality using the familiar chivalric plot of the perilous journey of the young knight to the castle of his lady. The philosophy of the play relates to that of St. Thomas More and his circle.

Other "youth" plays:

> *Glass of Government* (No. XIII).
> *Hickscorner* (No. XVI).
> *Lusty Juventus* (No. XXX).

Marriage of Wit and Wisdom (No. XXXIV).
Misogonus (No. XXXVI).
Nice Wanton (No. XLI).
Youth (No. LIX).
See the other "wit" plays:
Marriage of Wit and Science (No. XXXIII).
Marriage of Wit and Wisdom (No. XXXIV).

Critical Studies

Brown, Arthur. "The Play of *Wit and Science* by John Redford." *PQ*, 28:429-442 (1949).

Habicht, Werner. "The Wit-Interludes and the Form of Pre-Shakespearean 'Romantic Comedy'." *RenD*, 8:73-88 (1965).

Tannenbaum, Samuel. "Editorial Notes on *Wit and Science.*" *PQ*, 14:307-326 (1935).

Tomkins, Kenneth D. "The Wit Plays: Variations on a Tudor Dramatic Theme." *DA*, 28:3651A (1968).

Welz, John W. and Carl P. Daw, Jr. "Tradition and Originality in *Wyt and Science.*" *SP*, 65:631-646 (1968).

Withington, Robert. "Experience the Mother of Science." *PMLA*, 57:592 (1942).

LIX. YOUTH, 1513-29
(Anonymous)

Thēterlude of youth. John Waley, n.d.

Editions

J. O. Halliwell. *Contributions to Early English Literature,* 1849.
Dodsley, II.

W. Bang and R. B. McKerrow. *Materialien,* XII (1905).
*Farmer, 1906.

Dramatis Personae

Charity	Pride
Youth	Lechery
Humility	
Riot	

Length of the play: 820 lines.

Plot Summary
  Charity asserts his own importance in the scheme of salvation. He is rudely interrupted by impetuous Youth, who then boasts of his physical beauty and of the reckless life he leads. In spite of a threatened beating, Charity admonishes Youth, but finally decides to seek out his brother Humility for help. Youth next welcomes Riot, who, having escaped from Newgate, has just robbed a knight of twenty golden nobles. At Riot's invitation, they resolve to go to a tavern for drinking and wenching. Riot promises that if Charity and Humility come again he will personally put them in the stocks. He further protects his young protege by giving him Pride as a servant. Pride assumes the education in vice of Youth, instructs him in the art of self-aggrandizement, and procures Lady Lechery as Youth's mistress. When Charity attempts to prohibit their proceeding to the tavern, Riot and Pride bind him in chains where he patiently endures the temporary victory of the vices until Humility sets him free. Riot and Pride return from the tavern and confront the virtues for the soul of Youth. At first Youth will not forsake Pride, Riot, and the impetuous life he has been leading. But when Charity explains the redemption, Youth first forsakes Pride and then Riot. The play ends with an exhortation to men to mend their ways.

Comments

Youth should be studied along with *Hickscorner* (No. XVI), *Mankind* (No. XXXII), and *Mundus et Infans* (No. XXXVII). Evident in all these early moralities is the concern of the older generation over the disrespectful, over-indulged younger set.

Other "youth" plays:

> *Glass of Government* (No. XIII).
> *Lusty Juventus* (No. XXX).
> *Marriage of Wit and Wisdom* (No. XXXIV).
> *Misogonus* (No. XXXVI).
> *Nice Wanton* (No. XLI).
> *Wit and Science* (No. LVIII).

Critical Studies

Schell, E. T. *"Youth* and *Hyckesorner:* Which Came First?" *PQ,* 45:468-474 (1966).

Appendix I

COMING OF DEATH

The Coming of Death (or Summons of Death) was an important theme of literature and art in the late Middle Ages. Authors and artists alike devoted their talents to a realistic depiction of the physical effects of death in all their terrible detail. The medieval view of death was not unilateral. Everyone in the Middle Ages saw easily and clearly, however painfully, to the other side of death, where Heaven was the eternal reward for those who died in the state of grace and hell was the punishment for those who died with unrepented mortal sin on their souls. One important aspect of this theme, although it does not appear in the English moralities, is the Danse Macabre.

The Coming of Death is found in the following English moralities:

The Castle of Perseverance, II. 2779 ff. Death enters, boasts of his lordship over the whole world, and strikes Humanum Genus down with his dart. See No. V.

Ludus Coventriae, ed. K. S. Block, *EETS,* Extra Series, cxx, London, 1917 (Reprinted in 1961), p. 176. Here Mors visits the drunken Herod who is received by the Devil. (*Ludus Coventriae* is a mystery not a morality).

Pride of Life. The entire action of this fragmentary play is taken up with the Coming of Death. See No. XLIII.

Everyman. Like *Pride of Life,* the action of *Everyman* is totally devoted to the Coming of Death. See No. XII.

Other allegorical figures who take on a role in the later moralities similar to that of Death:

Adversity in *Magnificence.* See No. XXXI.

Divine Correction in the *Satire of the Three Estates.* See No. XLV.

Nemesis in *Respublica.* Se. No. XLIV.

God's Visitation in the *Trial of Treasure.* See No. LIII.

Correction in *Tide Tarrieth No Man.* See No. LI.

167

Horror in *Conflict of Conscience*. No. IX.
Rumor in *Nice Wanton*. Se. No. XLI.
God's Judgment in *The Longer Thou Livest the More Fool Thou Art*. See No. XXVI.
God's Plague in *Enough is as Good as a Feast*. See No. XI.
Severity in *Like Will to Like*. See No. XXV.
Justice and Reward in *Appius and Virginia*. See No. III.

Critical Studies

Hammond, Eleanor P. *English Verse between Chaucer and Surrey*. Durham, N. C.: University of North Carolina Press, 1927, pp. 124-130. (Reprinted, New York: Octagon Books, 1969).

Spencer, Theodore. *Death and Elizabethan Tragedy*. Cambridge, Mass.: Harvard University Press, 1936, pp. 21-34. (Reprinted, New York: Pageant Books, 1960).

Spivack, Bernard. *Shakespeare and the Allegory of Evil*. New York: Columbia University Press, 1958, pp. 63-67.

Appendix II

DEBATE OF THE BODY AND SOUL

Like the Coming of Death, the Debate of the Body and Soul was a major theme of literature in the Middle Ages. The Soul blames the Body which has been addicted to ease and pleasure while living. The Body looks back longingly to youth when it was given to luxury and accuses the Soul for its present state of decay.

There are too many treatments of this theme outside the drama to mention them here. A literary bibliography will be found in the usual sources such as the Wells *Manual,* pp. 411-413 and Supplements; Baugh, *A Literary History of England,* pp. 162-164; and the *MLA Bibliography.*

Only two of the earliest extant English moralities have this theme:

The Pride of Life, 11. 93-100. These lines are part of the Prologue to the play. They naturally do not give the actual debate, but inform the spectators that it will take place later on. Unfortunately, the fragment breaks off before this episode. See No. XLIII.

The Castle of Perseverance, 11. 3013-3021. See No. V.

Critical Studies

Allison, Tempe E. "On the Body and Soul Legend." *MLN,* 42:102-106 (1927).

Spivack, Bernard. *Shakespeare and the Allegory of Evil.* New York: Columbia University Press (1958) pp. 63-64, 67-69.

Appendix III
DEBATE OF THE HEAVENLY GRACES or THE PARLIAMENT IN HEAVEN

The Four Daughters of God (or the Four Heavenly Graces) debate before the throne of God the salvation or damnation of humanity after the fall of Adam. Justice and Truth argue for the strict interpretation of the law, whereas Mercy pleads for man's salvation. God decides in favor of Mercy, and Peace restores harmony between the debaters. It is decided that the Second Person of the Blessed Trinity, God the Son, will descend to earth to redeem man.

The following are early versions of the Debate outside the drama:

Grosseteste, Robert. *Carmina Anglo-Normannica,* ed. Matthew Cooke. Caxton Society, London, 1852. This volume contains both the *Chasteau d'Amour* and its English counterpart *The Castel of Love.*

Cursor Mundi, ed. Richard Morris, *EETS,* Old Series, lvii (1874), lix (1875), lxii (1876), lxvi (1877), lxviii (1878), ci (1893), ll. 9517-9752.

The Mirrour of the Blessed Lyf of Jesu Christ, ed. Lawrence F. Powell, Roxburghe Club, Oxford (1908) pp. 14-19. This is a translation by Nicholas Love of the *Meditationes Vitae Christi* of Bonaventure, a cardinal of Padua.

Gesta Romanorum, ed. Sidney Herrtage. *EETS,* Extra Series, xxxiii, London (1879) pp. 132-135.

Piers Plowman, ed. Skeat. B-text, XVIII, ll. 110 ff.; C-text, XXI, ll. 115 ff.

John Lydgate. *The Court of Sapience,* ed. Robert Spinder. Beiträge zur englischen Philologie, VI (1927), ll. 176 ff.

The Debate of the Heavenly Graces in English drama:

Ludus Coventriae, ed. K. S. Block. *EETS,* Extra Series, cxx, London, 1917 (Reprinted in 1961), pp. 97-103. The Debate occurs before the Annunciation.

The Castle of Perseverance, 11. 3130 ff. This is the finest example of the Debate in the English moralities. See. No V.

Mankind, 11. 832-832. See No. XXXII.

Hickscorner, 11. 119-20. The allusion to the Debate is not as clear as it is in *Mankind.* See No. XVI.

Processus Satanae, ed. W. W. Greg. *Malone Society Collections II, 3.* London (1931) pp. 239-250.

Respublica, 11. 1866 ff. See No. XLIV.

Critical Studies

Traver, Hope. *The Four Daughters of God.* Bryn Mawr: Bryn Mawr College Monographs, 1907.

Chew, Samuel. *The Virtues Reconciled; an Iconographic Study.* Toronto: University of Toronto Press, 1947.

Appendix IV

THE DEVIL IN THE MORALITIES

Called Belial, Lucifer, or Satan, the Devil appears in nine moralities:

The Castle of Perseverance, one of the Three Evil Powers (the World, the Flesh, the Devil). See No. V.

Wisdom, the Devil takes an active role in the tempting of Anima. This is the only morality in which the Devil enjoys a significant role. See No. LVII.

Digby *Mary Magdalene,* one of the Three Evil Powers. See No. XXXV.

Lusty Juventus, the Devil calls forth the Vice Hypocrisy to work against the Reformation. See No. XXX.

Conflict of Conscience, Satan appears in the Prologue. See No. IX.

Enough is as Good as a Feast, the Devil carries Worldly Man to hell on his back. See No. XI.

Like Will to Like, the Devil commissions the Vice Nichol Newfangle. See No. XXV.

Virtuous and Godly Susanna, the Devil commissions the Vice Ill Report. See No. LIV.

All for Money, the Devil commissions the Vice Sin. See No. II.

Critical Studies

Allison, T. E. "The *Paternoster Play* and the Origin of the Vice." *PMLA,* 39:789-804 (1924).

Chambers, E. K. *The Medieval Stage.* 2 vols. London: Oxford University Press, 1903.

Cushman, L. W. *The Devil and the Vice in English Dramatic Literature.* Halle: M. Niemeyer, 1900.

Mares, Francis Hugh. "The Origin of the Figure called 'the Vice' in Tudor Drama." *HLQ,* 22:11-29 (1958).

Spivack, Bernard. *Shakespeare and the Allegory of Evil.* New

York: Columbia University Press (1958), Chapter V. Emergence of the Vice, pp. 131-150.

Withington, Robert. "The Ancestry of the 'Vice'." *Speculum,* 7:525-529 (1932).

_____ "Braggart, Devil and 'Vice,' A Note on the Development of Comic Figures in the Early English Drama." *Speculum,* 11:124-129 (1936).

_____ "The Development of the 'Vice'." In *Essays in Memory of Barrett Wendell by His Assistants.* Cambridge, Mass.: Harvard University Press (1926), pp. 153-167.

Appendix V

THE PSYCHOMACHIA
(Prudentius)

Written by Prudentius in the fourth century, the *Psycho-machia* derives its form from the epic and its content from a theme as old as the human race — the militantly contrary natures of good and evil, of virtue and vice. The characters of the epic are virtues and vices personified as warriors; their battlefield is humanity; their cause is the possession of the soul of each and every man. There are in all, seven stages in the terrible contest of vice and virtue of which Prudentius speaks. In each stage a virtue unmercifully destroys an opposing vice in pitched battle. The stages are as follows: Fides vs Veterum Cultura Deorum; Puditia vs Sodomita Libido; Patientia vs Ira; Mens Humilis vs Superbia; Sobrietas vs Luxuria; Operatio vs Avaritia; Concordia vs Discordia.

The action of the sixth stage is important for it was to be repeated time and again in the moralities and later Elizabethan and Jacobean drama. In it Avaritia, undismayed by the failure of the other vices in open attack against the virtues, becomes the first of a legion of vice-intriguers. She disguises herself as Thrift, and, by means of artful dissimulation, succeeds in undermining the forces of good until Operatio (Good Works) both stabs and chokes her to death.

The most thorough treatment of the *Psychomachia* and its relation to the drama is Chapter Three of Bernard Spivack's *Shakespeare and the Allegory of Evil* (New York: Columbia University Press, 1958) pp. 60-95.

The following may also be useful:

Bloomfield, M. W. "A Source of Prudentius' *Psychomachia.*" *Speculum,* 18:87-90 (1943).

Cerri, A. "Aspetti di polemica antimitologica e di composizione poetica in Prudenzio." *Athenaeum,* 42:334-360 (1964).

Cotagni, L. "Sovrapposizione di visione e di allegorie nella

174

Psychomachia di Prudenzio." Rendiconti della Accademia
Nazionale dei Lincei, Classe di Scienze Morali, Storiche e
Filologiche. Series VI, Vol. 12 (1936), pp. 441-461.

Deferrari, R. J. and J. M. Cambell. *A Concordance of
Prudentius.* Cambridge, Mass.: The Medieval Academy of
America, 1932.

Gnilka, Christian. *Studien zur Psychomachie des Prudentius.*
Klassischphilologische Studien. XXVII. Wiesbaden:
Harrassowitz, 1963.

Hench, Atcheson. "Sources of Prudentius' *Psychomachia.*"
CP, 19:78-80 (1924).

Herzog, R. *Die allegorische Dichtkunst des Prudentius.*
Zetemata, Monographien zur klassischen Altertumswissen-
schaft. XLII. Munich: Beck, 1966.

Jauss, H. J. *Form und Auffassung der Allegorie in der Tradition der Psychomachia.* Medium Aevum Vivum. Festschrift fur W. Bulst, Heidelberg, 1960.

Katzenellenbogen, Adolf. *Allegories of the Virtues and Vices
in Medieval Art.* London: The Warburg Institute, 1939.

Lavarenne, _____ . *Etude sur la lange du poète Prudence.*
Paris, 1933.

Lubac, H. de. "A propos de l'allégorie chrétienne." *Recher-
ches de Science Religieuse,* 47:5-43 (1959).

Peebles, B. M. *The Poet Prudentius.* New York: McMullen
Books, 1951.

The Poems of Prudentius: Apologetic and Didactic Poems,
Vol II. trans. Sister Mary Clement Eagan. Washington,
D. C.: The Catholic University of America Press, 1965.

The Works of Prudentius. 2 vols. trans. H. J. Thomson. Cambridge, Mass.: Loeb Classical Library, 1953-62.

Thomson, H. J. "The *Psychomachia* of Prudentius." *CR,*
44:109-112 (1930).

Appendix VI
STAGING OF MORALITY PLAYS

Arnott, Peter. "The Origin of Medieval Theatre in the Round." *TN,* 15:84-87 (1961).

Bevington, David. *From Mankind to Marlowe.* Cambridge, Mass.: Harvard University Press, 1962.

Chambers. E. K. *The Elizabethan Stage.* 4 vols. Oxford: The Clarendon Press, 1923.

_____ *The Medieval Stage.* 2 vols. London: Oxford University Press, 1903.

Collins, Fletcher. "The Relation of Tudor Halls to Elizabethan Public Theatres." *PQ,* 10:313-316 (1931).

Craik, T. W. *The Tudor Interlude.* Leicester: The University Press, 1967.

Dodd, Kenneth M. "Another Elizabethan Theatre in the Round." *SQ,* 21:125-156 (1970).

Fifield, Merle. *The Castle in the Circle.* Ball State Monograph 6. Muncie, Ind.: Ball State University Press, 1967.

Hosley, Richard. "Three Kinds of Outdoor Theatre before Shakespeare." *ThS,* 12:125-156 (1970).

Kernodle, George. *From Art to Theatre: Form and Convention in the Renaissance.* Chicago: University of Chicago Press, 1944.

McDowell, John H. "Tudor Court Staging: A Study in Perspective." *JEGP,* 44:194-207 (1945).

Murray, John T. *English Dramatic Companies, 1558-1642.* 2 vols. Boston: Houghton Mifflin, 1910. (Reprinted, New York: Russell and Russell, 1963).

Nicoll, Allardyce. *The Development of the Theatre.* 5th ed. rev. New York: Harcourt, Brace, 1966.

Richter, Bodo L. "Recent Studies in Renaissance Scenography." *RN,* 19:344-358 (1966).

Schmitt, Natalie C. "Was There a Medieval Theatre in the Round? A Re-evaluation of the Evidence (Part I)." *TN,* 23:130-142 (1969). Part II, *TN,* 24:18-25 (1970).

176

Southern, Richard. "The Contribution of the Interludes to
   Elizabethan Staging." In *Essays on Shakespeare and the
   Elizabethan Drama in Honor of Hardin Craig.* Columbia,
   Mo.: University of Missouri Press (1962), pp. 3-14.
   _____ *The Medieval Theatre in the Round.* London:
   Faber and Faber, 1957.
Wickham, Glynne. *Early English Stages 1300-1660.* 2 vols.
   New York: Columbia University Press, 1959-63.
Young, Karl. *The Drama of the Medieval Church.* 2 vols.
   Oxford: The Clarendon Press, 1933.

GENERAL BIBLIOGRAPHY
OF THE MORALITY DRAMA

Allen, James S. "Changes in the Structure and Characterization of the English Moral Play after 1516." *DA*, 14:1404 (1954).

Allison, T. E. "On the Body and Soul Legend." *MLN*, 42:102-106 (1927).

_____ "The *Paternoster Play* and the Origin of the Vice." *PMLA*, 39:789-804 (1924).

Arnott, Peter. "The Origins of Medieval Theatre in the Round." *TN*, 15:84-87 (1961).

Baskervill, C. R. *The Elizabethan Jig, and Related Song Drama.* Chicago: University of Chicago Press, 1929.

Bernard, J. E. *Prosody of the Tudor Interlude.* New Haven: Yale University Press, 1939.

Bevington, David. "Drama and Polemics under Queen Mary." *RenD*, 9:105-124 (1966).

_____ *From Mankind to Marlowe.* Cambridge, Mass.: Harvard University Press, 1962.

_____ *Tudor Drama and Politics.* Cambridge, Mass.: Harvard University Press, 1968.

Blackburn, Ruth Harriett. "Tudor Biblical Drama." *DA*, 17:1746-1747 (1957).

Bloomfield, Morton. *The Seven Deadly Sins: An Introduction to the History of a Religious Concept with Special Reference to Medieval English Literature.* East Lansing, Michigan: Michigan State College Press, 1952.

Boas, F. S. "*The Four Cardynall Vertues,* a Fragmentary Moral Interlude." *QQ,* 58:85-91 (1951).

_____ *An Introduction to Tudor Drama.* Oxford: The Clarendon Press, 1933.

_____ *University Drama in the Tudor Age.* Oxford: The Clarendon Press, 1914.

Borchardt, Donald Arthur. "The Dramatic Nature of the English Morality Play." *DA*, 21:3553 (1961).

Bradner, Leicester. "The Rise of Secular Drama in the Renaissance." *SRen*, 3:7-22 (1956).

Brandl, Alois. *Quellen des weltlichen Dramas in England vor Shakespeare.* In Quellen und Forschungen zur Sprach und Culturgeschichte des germanischen Volker, LXXX. Strassburg, 1898.

Brooke, C. F. Tucker. *The Tudor Drama.* Boston: Houghton and Mifflin, 1911.

Brooks, N. C. "Latin Morality Dialogues of the 15th Century." *JEGP*, 42:471-474 (1943).

Calderhead, I. G. "Morality Fragments from Norfolk." *MP*, 14:1-9 (1916).

Chambers, E. K. *The Elizabethan Stage.* 4 vols. Oxford: The Clarendon Press, 1923.

_____ *The Medieval Stage.* 2 vols. Oxford: The Clarendon Press, 1903.

Chew, Samuel. *The Virtues Reconciled; an Iconographic Study.* Toronto: University of Toronto Press, 1947.

Clough, Wilson O. "The Broken English of Foreign Characters on the Elizabethan Stage." *PQ,* 12:255-268. (1933).

Collier, John Payne. *A History of English Dramatic Poetry to the Time of Shakespeare.* 3 vols. London: G. Bell and Sons, 1879.

Collins, Fletcher. "The Relation of Tudor Halls to Elizabethan Public Theatres." *PQ,* 10:313-316 (1931).

Collins, Sister Mary Emmanuel. "The Allegorical Motifs in the Early English Moral Plays." Yale University Dissertation, 1936.

Craig, Hardin. *English Religious Drama of the Middle Ages.* Oxford: The Clarendon Press, 1955.

_____ "Morality Plays and Elizabethan Drama." *SQ,* 1:64-72 (1950).

Craik, T. W. *The Tudor Interlude.* Leicester: University of Leicester Press, 1958.

Creizenach, Wilhelm. *Geschichte des neueren Dramas.* vols. I-III. Halle, 1893-1903.

Cushman, Lysander W. *The Devil and the Vice in English Dramatic Literature before Shakespeare.* Halle: S. M. Niemeyer, 1900.

Dessen, Alan C. "The 'Estates' Morality Play." *SP,* 62:121-136 (1965).

_____ "The Morall as an Elizabethan Dramatic Kind." *CD,* 5:138-159 (1971).

Dodd, Kenneth M. "Another Elizabethan Theatre in the Round." *SQ,* 21:125-156 (1970).

Dodds, Madeleine. "Early Political Plays." *The Library,* 3rd ser. 4:393-408 (1913).

Eckhardt, Eduard. *Die lustige Person in älteren englischen Drama.* Berlin: Mayer and Muller, 1902.

_____ "Die metrische Unterscheidung von Ernst und Komik in den englischen Moralitäten." *EngSt,* 62:152-169 (1927).

Farnham, Willard. *The Medieval Heritage of Elizabethan Tragedy.* Berkeley, Calif.: University of California Press, 1936.

Fifield, Merle. *The Castle in the Circle.* Ball State Monograph 6. Muncie, Ind.: Ball State University Press, 1967.

Flood, W. H. Grattan. "Early Tudor Drama." *RES,* 3:445-446 (1927).

Gardner, Harold C. *Mysteries' End: An Investigation of the Last Days of the Medieval Religious Stage.* New Haven: Yale University Press, 1946.

Graves, T. S. "Some Allusions to Religious and Political Plays." *MP*, 9:545-554 (1912).

Greg, W. W. "Authorship Attributions in the Early Play-Lists." Edinburgh: *Transactions of the Bibliographical Society*, II, 305-329 (1946).

_____ *A Bibliography of the English Printed Drama to the Restoration.* 4 vols. London: The Bibliographical Society, 1939-59.

_____ *A List of English Plays Written Before 1643 and Printed before 1700.* London: The Bibliographical Society, 1900.

Griffin, William J. "Notes on Early Tudor Control of the Stage." *MLN*, 58:50-54 (1943).

Habicht, Werner. *Studien zur Dramenform vor Shakespeare: Moralität, Interlude, Romaneskes Drama."* Anglistische Forschungen, 96, Heidelberg: Carl Winter, 1968.

Halliwell-Philips, James O. *A Dictionary of Old English Plays in Print or in Manuscript.* 2 vols. London: J. R. Smith, 1860. (Reprinted, Naarden: A. W. Bekhoven, 1968).

Happé, P. "The Vice and Folk Drama." *Folklore*, 75:161-193 (1964).

Harbage, Alfred. *Annals of English Drama, 975-1700.* Philadelphia: University of Pennsylvania Press, 1940. Revised: S. Schoenbaum (London, 1964).

Harvey, Florence H. "The Morality Play in the Development of English Drama." *Dial*, 34:296-297 (1903).

Hazlitt, William Carew. *The English Drama and Stage under the Tudor and Stuart Princes, 1543-1664.* London: The Roxburghe Library, 1869. (Reprinted, New York: B. Franklin, 1969).

_____ *Handbook to the Popular Poetical and Dramatic Literature of Great Britain from the Invention of Printing to the Restoration.* London: J. R. Smith, 1867.

_____ *A Manual for the Collector and Amateur of Old English Plays.* London: Pickering and Chatto, 1892. (Reprinted, New York: Johnson Reprint Corp., 1967).

Henslowe, Philip. *Henslowe's Diary.* Ed. R. A. Foakes and R. T. Rickert. Cambridge: Cambridge University Press, 1961.

Hillebrand, H. N. *The Child Actors.* 2 vols. Urbana, Ill.: University of Illinois Press, 1926. (Reprinted, New York: Russell and Russell, 1964).

Hogrefe, Pearl. *The Sir Thomas More Circle.* Urbana, Ill.: University of Illinois Press, 1959.

Holzknecht, K. J. *Outlines of Tudor and Stuart Plays, 1497-1642.* New York: Barnes and Noble, 1947.

Hosley, Richard. "Three Kinds of Outdoor Theatre before Shakespeare." *ThS*, 12:125-156 (1970).

Huganir, Kathryn. "Medieval Theatres." *TA*, 23:34-45 (1968).

Huizinga, Johan. *The Waning of the Middle Ages*. London: E. Arnold, 1924.

Iwasaki, Soji. "The Changing Ideas of Time and the Timeless in English Morality Plays." *SELit*, 46:1-17 (1969).

Johnson, R. C. "Audience Involvement in the Tudor Interlude." *TN*, 24:101-111 (1970).

Katzenellenbogen, Adolf. *Allegories of the Virtues and Vices in Medieval Art*. London: The Warburg Institute, 1939.

Kernodle, George. *From Art to Theatre: Form and Convention in the Renaissance*. Chicago: University of Chicago Press, 1944.

Kinghorn, A. M. *Medieval Drama*. London: Evans Brothers Limited, 1968.

Kurtz, L. P. *The Dance of Death and the Macabre Spirit in European Literature*. New York: Publications of the Institute of French Studies of Columbia University, 1934.

Lawrence, William J. "The Practice of Doubling and Its Influence on Early Dramaturgy." In *Pre-Restoration Stage Studies*. Cambridge, Mass.: Harvard University Press (1927), pp. 43-78.

Leigh, D. J. "The Doomsday Mystery Play: An Eschatological Morality." *MP*, 67:211-223 (1970).

Lombardo, Agostino. *Il dramma pre-shakespeariano: studi sul teatro inglese dal Medioevo al Rinascimento*. Venice, 1957.

MacKenzie, W. R. *The English Moralities from the Viewpoint of Allegory*. Boston: Ginn and Company, 1914.

_____ "The Origin of the English Morality." *Washington University Studies, Humanistic Series 4*, 2:141-164 (1915).

Mares, Francis Hugh. "The Origin of the Figure Called 'the vice' in Tudor Drama." *HLQ*, 22:11-29 (1958).

Margeson, J. M. R. *The Origins of English Tragedy*. Oxford: The Clarendon Press, 1967.

Martin, Jo Ann. "The Secularization of the English Morality Play." *DA*, 24:3326 (1964).

Maxwell, Ian. *French Farce and John Heywood*. Melbourne: Melbourne University Press, 1946.

McCollom, William G. "From Dissonance to Harmony: The Evolution of Early English Comedy." *TA*, 21:69-96 (1964).

McCutchan, J. Wilson. "Justice and Equity in the English Morality Play." *JHI*, 19:405-410 (1958).

_____ "Personified Abstractions as Characters in Elizabethan Dramas." University of Virginia Dissertation, 1949.

McDowell, John H. "Tudor Court Staging: A Study in Perspective." *JEGP*, 44:194-207 (1945).

182

Mill, Anna J. *Medieval Plays in Scotland*. London: W. Blackwood and Sons, 1927. (Reprinted, New York: B. Blom, 1969).

Mohl, Ruth. *The Three Estates in Medieval and Renaissance Literature*. New York: Columbia University Press, 1933. (Reprinted, New York: F. Ungar, 1962).

Moore, E. Hamilton. *English Miracle Plays and Moralities*. London: Sherratt and Hughes, 1907 (Reprinted, New York, AMS Press, 1969).

Moore, John Robert. "Ancestors of Autolycus in the English Moralities and Interludes." *Washington University Studies, Humanistic Series*, 9:157-164 (1922).

Motter, T. H. V. *The School Drama in England*. London: Langman's, 1929. (Reprinted, Port Washington, N. Y.: Kennikat Press, 1968).

Murray, John T. *English Dramatic Companies, 1558-1642*. 2 vols. Boston: Houghton and Mifflin, 1910 (Reprinted, New York: Russell and Russell, 1963).

Nicoll, Allardyce. *The Development of the Theatre*. 5th ed., rev. New York: Harcourt, Brace, 1966.

_____ *Masks, Mimes, and Miracles: Studies in the Popular Theatre*. New York: Harcourt, Brace, 1931. (Reprinted, New York: Cooper Square Publishers, 1963).

Owst, G. R. *Literature and Pulpit in Medieval England*. 2nd ed., rev. New York: Barnes and Noble, 1961.

Peake, Richard H. "The Stage Prostitute in the English Dramatic Tradition from 1558-1625." *DA*, 27:3847A-3848A (1967).

Pineas, Rainer. "The English Morality Play as a Weapon of Religious Controversy." *SEL*, 2:157-180 (1962).

Pollard, A. W. and G. R. Redgrave. *A Short-Title Catalogue of Books Printed in England, Scotland, and Ireland and of English Books Printed Abroad, 1475-1640*. London: The Bibliographical Society, 1926.

Potter, Robert Alonza. "The Form and Content of the English Morality Play." *DA*, 26:7323-7324 (1961).

Prater, Neal B. "The Origin of the English Tragicomedy and Its Development before Shakespeare." *DA*, 28:4141A-4142A (1968).

The Works of Prudentius. 2 vols. trans. H. J. Thomson. Cambridge Mass.: Loeb Classical Library, 1953, 1962.

Ramsay, Robert L. *Introduction to Skelton's Magnyfycence*. London: Publications of the Early English Text Society, Extra Series, xcviii, 1906.

Reed, Arthur W. *The Beginnings of the English Secular and Romantic Drama*. Shakespeare Association Pamphlet 7, Oxford: Oxford University Press, 1922.

_____ *Early Tudor Drama: Medwall, the Rastells, Heywood, and the More Circle.* London: Methuen, 1926. (Reprinted, New York: Octagon Books, 1969).

Ribner, Irving. "Morality Roots of the Tudor History Play." *TSE,* 4:21-44 (1954).

_____ *Tudor and Stuart Drama.* Goldentree Bibliographies. New York: Appleton-Century-Crofts, 1966.

Richter, Bodo L. "Recent Studies in Renaissance Scenography." *RN,* 19:344-358 (1966).

Roberts, Morris. "A Note on the Sources of the English Morality Play." *Studies by Members of the Department of English, University of Wisconsin,* 18:100-117 (1923).

Robinson, J. W. "Three Notes on Medieval Theatre." *TN,* 16:60-62 (1962).

Rossiter, A. P. *English Drama from Early Times to the Elizabethans.* London: Hutchinson, 1950.

Roston, Murray. *Biblical Drama in England from the Middle Ages to the Present Day.* London: Faber and Faber, 1968.

Russell, H. K. "Tudor and Stuart Dramatizations of the Doctrines of Natural and Moral Philosophy." *SP,* 31:1-27 (1934).

Schelling, Felix E. *Elizabethan Drama 1558-1642.* 2 vols. Boston: Houghton and Mifflin, 1908.

_____ *Elizabethan Playwrights: A Short History of the English Drama from Medieval Times to the Closing of the Theatres in 1642.* New York: Harper, 1925.

Schmitt, Natalie C. "Was There a Medieval Theatre in the Round? A Re-evaluation of the Evidence (Part I)." *TN,* 23:130-142 (1969). Part II, *TN,* 24:18-25 (1970).

Shuchter, Julian D. "Man Redeemable, the Mankind Character in the English Morality Plays: A Study in Theatre and Theology." *DA,* 29:3156A (1969).

Sibley, Gertrude M. *The Lost Plays and Masques, 1500-1642.* Ithaca: Cornell University Press, 1933.

Southern, Richard. "The Contribution of the Interludes to Elizabethan Staging." In *Essays on Shakespeare and the Elizabethan Drama in Honor of Hardin Craig.* Columbia, Mo.: University of Missouri Press (1962), pp. 3-14.

_____ "Les Interludes au temps des Tudor." In *Le Lien théâtral de la Renaissance.* Paris: Editions du Centre National de La Recherche Scientifique, 1964.

_____ *The Medieval Theatre in the Round.* London: Faber and Faber, 1957.

Spivack, Bernard. *Shakespeare and the Allegory of Evil.* New York: Columbia University Press, 1958.

Spivack, Charlotte. "The Comedy of Evil in Medieval Art and Literature." *Cresset,* 22:8-15 (1963).

_____ "The Elizabethan Theatre: Circle and Center." *CentR,* 13:424-443 (1969).

Steele, Mary S. *Plays and Masques at Court during the Reigns of Elizabeth, James, and Charles.* New Haven: Yale University Press, 1926.

Stratman, Carl J. *Bibliography of Medieval Drama.* Berkeley and Los Angeles: University of California Press, 1954.

Thompson, E. N. S. *The English Moral Play.* Publications of the Connecticut Academy of Arts and Sciences, 14:291-414 (1910).

Tobin, Terence. "The Beginnings of Drama in Scotland." *ThS,* 8:1-16 (1967).

Throp, Willard. *The Triumph of Realism in Elizabethan Drama, 1558-1612.* Princeton: Princeton University Press, 1928. (Reprinted, New York: Haskell House, 1965).

Traver, Hope. *The Four Daughters of God.* Bryn Mawr: Bryn Mawr College Monographs, 1907.

Wallace, Charles W. *The Evolution of the English Drama up to Shakespeare.* Berlin: G. Reimer, 1912.

Wellwarth, George E. "From Ritual to Drama: The Social Background of the Early English Theatre." *JGE,* 19:297-328 (1968).

Wharey, J. B. "Bunyan's Holy War and the Conflict Type of Morality Play." *MLN,* 34:65-73 (1919).

White, Helen C. *Social Criticism in Popular Religious Literature of the Sixteenth Century.* New York: Macmillan, 1944.

Whiting, Bartlett J. *Proverbs in the Earlier English Drama.* Cambridge, Mass.: Harvard University Press, 1938 (Reprinted, New York: Octagon Books, 1969).

Wickham, Glynne. *Early English Stages 1300-1660.* 2 vols. New York: Columbia University Press, 1959-63.

_____ *Shakespeare's Dramatic Heritage: Collected Studies in Medieval, Tudor, and Shakespearean Drama.* New York: Barnes and Noble, 1969.

Williams, Arnold. *The Drama of Medieval England.* East Lansing: Michigan State University Press, 1961.

_____ "The English Moral Play before 1500." *AnM,* 4:5-22 (1963).

Williams, Marilyn. "The Tudor Interlude 1495-1601: A Literary Historical Survey." *DA,* 28:4652A (1968).

Wilson, F. P. *The English Drama 1485-1585.* Oxford: The Clarendon Press, 1969.

Winslow, Ola E. *Low Comedy as a Structural Element in English Drama from the Beginnings to 1642.* Chicago: University of Chicago Libraries, 1926.

Withington, Robert. "The Ancestry of the 'Vice'." *Speculum*, 7:525-529 (1932).

_____ "Braggart, Devil and 'Vice,' A Note on the Development of Comic Figures in the Early English Drama." *Speculum*, 11:124-129 (1936).

_____ "The Development of the 'Vice'." In *Essays in Memory of Barrett Wendell by His Assistants.* Cambridge, Mass.: Harvard University Press (1926) pp. 153-167.

_____ "Vice and Parasite; A note on the Evolution of the Elizabethan Villain." *PMLA*, 49:743-751 (1934).

Wright, Celeste T. "Some Conventions Regarding the Usurer in Elizabethan Literature." *SP*, 31:176-197 (1934).

Wright, Louis B. "Social Aspects of Some Belated Moralities." *Anglia*, 54:107-148 (1930).

Yamada, Akihiro. "A Checklist of English Printed Drama Before 1641 at the Library of the University of Illinois." *RORD*, 11:31-53 (1968).

Young, Karl. *The Drama of the Medieval Church.* 2 vols; Oxford: The Clarendon Press, 1933.

ADDENDUM

Feldman, Sylvia D. *The Morality-Patterned Comedy of the Renaissance.* The Hague: Mouton, 1970.

Loomis, Roger Sherman. "Lincoln as a Dramatic Centre," in *Melanges d'Histoire du Theatre offerts a Gustave Cohen.* Paris: Librairie Nizet, 1950.

Recordings: *THE FIRST STAGE:* English Drama from its beginnings to the 1580's. British Broadcasting Corporation. Directed by John Barton. (Available from Dover Publications).

Pride of Life	*Hickscorner*
Mary Magdalene (Digby)	*Magnyfycence*
Mind, Will and Understanding	*The Play of the Wether*
The Castell of Perseverance	*Nice Wanton*
Everyman	*Kynge Johan*
Mundus et Infans	

CHARACTER INDEX

The Character Index includes supernumeraries when they are particular personages, e.g. Jupiter, Niceness. The Index does not include miscellaneous characters when they have no significant role, e.g. Messengers, Servants, Lords Attendant. Aliases and assumed names under disguise are not given unless they are listed as separate characters in the dramatis personae. The Roman numeral following the name of the character indicates the number of the play in the *Survey*.

187